Editor-in-Chief and Founder:
  Lyndon H. LaRouche, Jr.
Editorial Board: *Lyndon H. LaRouche, Jr. , Helga
  Zepp-LaRouche, Robert Ingraham, Tony
  Papert, Gerald Rose, Dennis Small, Jeffrey
  Steinberg, William Wertz*
Co-Editors: *Robert Ingraham, Tony Papert*
Managing Editor: *Nancy Spannaus*
Technology: *Marsha Freeman*
Books: *Katherine Notley*
Ebooks: *Richard Burden*
Graphics: *Alan Yue*
Photos: *Stuart Lewis*
Circulation Manager: *Stanley Ezrol*

INTELLIGENCE DIRECTORS
Counterintelligence: *Jeffrey Steinberg, Michele
  Steinberg*
Economics: *John Hoefle, Marcia Merry Baker,
  Paul Gallagher*
History: *Anton Chaitkin*
Ibero-America: *Dennis Small*
Russia and Eastern Europe: *Rachel Douglas*
United States: *Debra Freeman*

INTERNATIONAL BUREAUS
Bogotá: *Miriam Redondo*
Berlin: *Rainer Apel*
Copenhagen: *Tom Gillesberg*
Houston: *Harley Schlanger*
Lima: *Sara Madueño*
Melbourne: *Robert Barwick*
Mexico City: *Gerardo Castilleja Chávez*
New Delhi: *Ramtanu Maitra*
Paris: *Christine Bierre*
Stockholm: *Ulf Sandmark*
United Nations, N.Y.C.: *Leni Rubinstein*
Washington, D.C.: *William Jones*
Wiesbaden: *Göran Haglund*

ON THE WEB
e-mail: eirns@larouchepub.com
www.larouchepub.com
www.executiveintelligencereview.com
www.larouchepub.com/eiw
Webmaster: *John Sigerson*
Assistant Webmaster: *George Hollis*
Editor, Arabic-language edition: *Hussein Askary*

EIR (ISSN 0273-6314) *is published weekly
(50 issues), by EIR News Service, Inc.,
P.O. Box 17390, Washington, D.C. 20041-0390.
(703) 777-9451*

European Headquarters: E.I.R. GmbH, Postfach
Bahnstrasse 9a, D-65205, Wiesbaden, Germany
Tel: 49-611-73650
Homepage: http://www.eirna.com
e-mail: eirna@eirna.com
Director: Georg Neudecker

Montreal, Canada: 514-461-1557

Denmark: EIR - Danmark, Sankt Knuds Vej 11,
basement left, DK-1903 Frederiksberg, Denmark.
Tel.: +45 35 43 60 40, Fax: +45 35 43 87 57. e-mail:
eirdk@hotmail.com.

Mexico City: EIR, Sor Juana Inés de la Cruz 242-2
Col. Agricultura C.P. 11360
Delegación M. Hidalgo, México D.F.
Tel. (5525) 5318-2301
eirmexico@gmail.com

Canada Post Publication Sales Agreement
#40683579

Postmaster: Send all address changes to *EIR*, P.O.
Box 17390, Washington, D.C. 20041-0390.

Signed articles in *EIR* represent the views of the
authors, and not necessarily those of the Editorial
Board.

Leadership for
A Nation in Turmoil

Leadership for a Nation in Turmoil

Feb. 7—Lyndon LaRouche addressed associates in these terms on Feb. 7.

I think the problem is, there is no will to solve the problem. The problem can be solved. First of all, the primary thing is that the financial system, the way it's operating now, is hopelessly bankrupt. Now, therefore, if the United States government were to foreclose against the fraudulent elements of investment, and just cancel them, we would have a solution. But the issue is that all the rich,— shall we say,— the rich demand that they have the first say in who gets paid and who does not. Well, if we say, we just cancelled all the pure speculators, who make no real contribution,— no physically meaningful progress,— then, if we got rid of them, we could handle the problem. And, in point of fact, not only is that a possibility, but unless we do that,— that is shut down the Obama administration on account of their frauds,— then we could all go down in chaos.

If we, on the other hand, are willing to admit reality . . . For example, we've got the case of Hillary and Sanders and so forth,— all those people who are in the campaign,— well, they're all worthless. They're all intrinsically worthless. What we have to do is cancel the worthless accounts, and build in a support system for funding which will allow us to create real productive steps. That can do it. And it can be done internationally. It can be done partly by help of Russia, in a very important political way; in China, with what China is building up around itself. All of these things are things which represent immediate forms of recovery of the global economy, just by simply cashing in and cancelling the trash. That's all we have to do. If we control the cash,— what is considered to be the cash. If we decide to do it, it will work. And when people say it won't work, it's because they've decided to cling to something worthless, like Wall Street. Wall Street and its organization is an intrinsically bankrupt institution. It has to be cancelled!

And if that were done with an understanding that we're doing that, that would solve the problem for the people of the United States and elsewhere.

Increasing Productive Powers of Labor

When people say they want this mysterious explanation of how the economy will work,— I am fully aware of what the standards are that are needed to solve the problem. I think that people are just ducking the issue, and hoping that there's some mysterious solution. The problem is that if people understand what I have been telling them for years,— and I've always been accurate on this one,— if they just pay attention to what I've been saying, and don't change the subject, we can deal with this thing. *We* can deal with it. But we are not the only force in play. I have the knowledge of how to deal with this problem. Others are trying to fish around and demanding an explanation of some unknown means of trying to solve the problem. I already know what the solution is. But I also know that the government, in its present form, is not willing, by any means, to save the economy. The government of the United States is not willing to tolerate,— not willing to deal with the issue which has to be applied. We don't need a mysterious explanation of how this thing can be dealt with. I'm fully aware of this, and I've been aware of this for years. But we've got to get back to what the real issue is. And the real issue is what our people, themselves, often try to avoid taking up, and then they hope that some mysterious force will actually provide a solution. It won't. I've been specifying that solution for years, and if you don't use that solution, you're wasting your time in trying to save anything.

The whole nation is bankrupt. The whole United States system is bankrupted entirely. Now, I could deal with that problem if I had the authority to do so, because I know exactly what I would have to cancel, and how I would have to cancel it, to get a viable United States economy. I know how to do that, and other people also do,— they know about it, but they don't dare to present the solution,— because somebody might be unhappy. Because we would have to strip down much of what is called the wealth area of the United States,— we would have to strip it down, because it has no intrinsic value. And we desperately need real value now. The reason people come up with other questions is because they're ducking the issue; they're denying reality. Reality is that you have to shut down Wall Street. Shut it down, flat, empty. Terminate it.

Then you have all these kinds things that go on which are listed as wealth matters, and they all are worthless. Most of Manhattan is full of worthlessness. But the people who want to have the wealth, or the appearance of wealth, will go around and demand special legislation, all kinds of things, to reward the useless. And that's what they do.

So the problem is when most people are talking about this issue, about how to deal with finances, they're just kidding themselves; they are blinding themselves to the fact that everything they're saying is damn silly. And we've got to get into reality. *We have to cancel worthless values, intrinsically worthless values.* We have to put people into productive work, and creative forces of work. You have to change things by dumping most of what passes for the official wealth of the rich. If you aren't willing to do that, you don't have a solution; you're just making it worse.

I've always been right on that, as against those who disagreed, or who had other ways of approaching it. You have to be productive, rather than speculative. People who have accepted other voices are rejecting what the meaning of income is, the productive kind of income and what it means. They have ignored that fact, or they give lip-service for it, but then they turn around immediately and try to avoid it.

What Is Leadership?

Those who are looking for other solutions are making fools of themselves; I know what the solution is. The solution is, you shut down Wall Street, and everything that represents Wall Street. Then Wall Street has no income. Why is that so? Because it's worthless.

But we refuse to do the things which will actually create wealth. The solution is the one that's being carried forward by Putin, himself, and by China, and by the nations which are coming together around cooperation with China, in economic and related matters. That works. What doesn't work is the trans-Atlantic region. The trans-Atlantic community is bankrupt, and it's based on financial systems which are intrinsically bankrupt. And therefore you have to change the way you function in terms of economy, to come back to a real economy, around an increase of the productive powers of labor. This doesn't mean being a socialist, and calling yourself a "laborer." This means that you have to create progress, per capita, per person, all the way through. Tomorrow has to be better than today, in terms of productivity, the powers of productivity. And people are not concerned about productivity. They're concerned about getting money. And that's where the problem comes up. We don't need money as such; that's not the solution; it's not a solution.

What you have to do is what Franklin Roosevelt did with his program, and that's the same thing. Of course, he was sabotaged when the right wing came in, and took over the majority. But what Franklin Roosevelt had done, in fact, before the crazy 1944 election, was a perfect conception of economic progress for the benefit of mankind. And anyone since then that doesn't agree with what I insist on in this, is an idiot. Or, they don't like to be called an idiot so they call themselves something else, but the fact is they're an idiot.

We've got to take what I've just said: that's the truth. And you've got to get yourself in accord with the truth.

MacArthur's Inchon landing decision was right, in lonely opposition to the whole government,— just as what I'm saying is right. I find myself often in that position, like the decision that confronted Douglas MacArthur. And I resonate with my memory of what he did, in terms of warfare and so forth. It's true: I have great respect for the memory of Douglas MacArthur, because Douglas MacArthur was the outstanding emblem of exactly what a nation in turmoil must do, as opposed to those who say there must be a practical solution. Whenever I hear that, I get angry, because you're selling yourselves out.

These are not abstract things or generalities; the point is that anything that wins, actually depends on decisions which provide the possibility to win. I know this thing cold; I know all the tricks about explanations and so forth,— it never works. You have to get creativity in effect; true creativity. Which is what I use as a measure for me every day of the week, every day of the year. Others want a practical solution; therefore they subtract from truth, rather than add to it.

I'm not just a figurehead; I'm committed all the way through, to what I represent. So I don't have any options,— different options. I don't have any.

EIR Contents

www.larouchepub.com Volume 43, Number 7, February 12, 2016

*Cover
This Week*

Kesha Rogers, a leader of the LaRouche PAC Policy Committee, was the Democratic nominee for Congress in Texas' 22nd District in 2010, as shown here, and again in 2012.

Correction: In *EIR*'s Feb. 5 issue, the correct image for China's high-temperature pebble bed demonstrator reactor at Roncheng City (page 35, in the "Dialogue from the *EIR* Forum, National Press Club") is shown here.

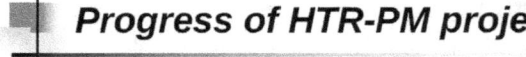

Progress of HTR-PM project

HTR-PM project location
Shidao Bay, Rongcheng City, Shandong Province, China.

HTR 2014

INET

I. Our Mission to the Stars

Kesha Rogers: 'This Is Something That We Really Have to Fight For'

Feb. 8—In this section, you, the reader, will find a series of articles which address the possibility of creating a new scientific Renaissance for the human species. This package, while not limited to these efforts, places a strong emphasis on the efforts now underway, particularly in China, to fulfill mankind's destiny in the stars. It is only fitting that we introduce this material with comments from Kesha Rogers, the LaRouche PAC leader who has battled unwaveringly for a revival of the U.S. Space program and a return to the vision of President John F. Kennedy. This is taken from her remarks to the Feb. 5, 2016 LaRouche PAC weekly webcast:

Kesha Rogers

Let me just make this point: this conception of the unique identity of the human species, evolving to change our conception and relationship to the universe in which we live, is something that Krafft Ehricke strongly believed in. And he called this conception, in his own words, man's "Extraterrestrial Imperative," and he developed this principle in his three core fundamental laws, which state:

1) Nobody and nothing under the natural laws of the Universe impose limitations on man, except man himself;

2) Not only the Earth, but the entire Solar System and as much of the Universe as he can reach under the laws of nature, are man's rightful field of activity;

3) By expanding through the Universe, man fulfills his destiny as an element of life, endowed with the power of reason, and wisdom, of the moral law within himself....

When you look at the fact that we have a completely insane policy, in terms of our election process, avoiding leadership, the fact is that no one is putting forward this vision, a real visionary policy of a national orientation of where we need to take this country, a national identity, which the Space program and President Kennedy inspired people with. This is something you should think about; this is something that we really have to fight for—that we have to restore a vision and we have to actually put this nation back on the road toward Progress. And the Space program is just what is necessary to do that.

China's Mission to Lunar Far Side Opens New Frontier for Mankind

by William Jones and Marsha Freeman

...If this capsule history of our progress teaches us anything, it is that man, in his quest for knowledge and progress, is determined and cannot be deterred. The exploration of space will go ahead, whether we join it or not, and it is one of the greatest adventures of all times, and no nation which expects to be the leader of other nations can expect to stay behind in this race for space.

—John F. Kennedy, speaking at Rice University, September 12, 1962

Feb. 6—China announced Jan. 14 that it was committed to landing a rover on the far side of the Moon in order to make *in situ* surveys of the lunar surface. In this way, China is on the verge of opening up a new frontier for mankind's exploration of the Galaxy. While China has only been a space-faring nation since the 1990s, its pace of development—as with China's economic development generally—has been mind boggling. While the United States, under George W. Bush, and even more under Barack Obama, has been dismantling space capabilities built up over four decades, China is proceeding by leaps and bounds, not just to repeat what other space-faring nations have done, but now to chart new paths.

The mission of Chang'e-4 to land on the far side of the Moon before 2020 is indeed going above and beyond what other nations have achieved.[1] "The implementation of the Chang'e-4 mission has helped our country make the leap from following to leading in the field of lunar exploration," said Liu Jizhong, chief of the lunar exploration center of the State Administration of Science, Technology and Industry for National Defense.

In fact, Chinese scientists decided at the start of their lunar exploration program that each new mission would break new ground. China's Chang'e-3 mission, which soft-landed the Yutu rover on the Moon in 2013—the first spacecraft to do so in almost 40 years—has taken the first deep subsurface lunar radar measurements ever, and made the first astronomical observations from the lunar surface. The latter were obtained with its ultraviolet telescope, called a "cosmic observatory." A second ultraviolet instrument will study Earth's ionosphere.

The next lunar mission, the Chang'e-5 craft,[2] now being developed for a 2017 launch, will be the star of an even more ambitious mission—landing on the Moon and then returning lunar samples to the Earth.

Mission to the Far Side

The follow-on Chang'e-4 mission to the far side of the Moon, to be launched before 2020, possibly as

2. Chang'e-5 will be launched before Chang'e-4.

Chinese National Space Administration

The Chang'e-4 relay satellite in this concept drawing from June 2015.

1. "Chang'e" is the name of the Moon goddess.

early as 2018, has generated great interest in the space science community. While the lunar far side was first photographed by Russia's Luna 4 spacecraft in 1959—and was seen and photographed by Apollo astronauts as they orbited the Moon—we have yet to investigate the soil and understand the evolutionary history of this mysterious, crater-filled landscape.

Because the far side of the Moon never faces Earth, due to its synchronous orbit,[3] the radio waves it receives from outer space can be detected without interference from the radio waves we produce on Earth. And the radio waves which cannot even be detected by ground-based radiotelescopes—since they do not penetrate Earth's ionosphere—will be detectable.

Speaking to the Yangguang network, Liu Jizhong said, "Chang'e-4 will utilize the distinctive features of the far side which are screened from the Earth's radio waves to develop a space science region in a forward position for a low frequency radio astronomy survey that hopefully will fill in some of the blanks in our knowledge."

The mission will study the geology and the dust features, and how they were formed. Liu explained, "Utilizing the very old rock of the lunar crust preserved on the far side of the Moon, we can investigate its geological characteristics, and hopefully by doing that, pull together for the first time a topographical configuration of the far side, its shallow structure, the composition of the lunar material of a particular cross-section, and attain a picture of its evolution, creating new knowledge about the history of the planet." Russian scientists have contributed a lunar dust surveyor.

The mission will also measure lunar surface residual magnetism and study its interaction with the solar

---

3. The Moon rotates on its axis as it orbits the Earth, but the far side never faces Earth. To understand this, consider that *you* are the Moon. As you orbit Earth, if you do *not* turn, you will alternately show your face and your backside to Earth. But you *could* politely turn as you go, always facing Earth. (But why does the Moon maintain this synchrony? Is it really a result of gravitational interaction with Earth?)

FIGURE 1

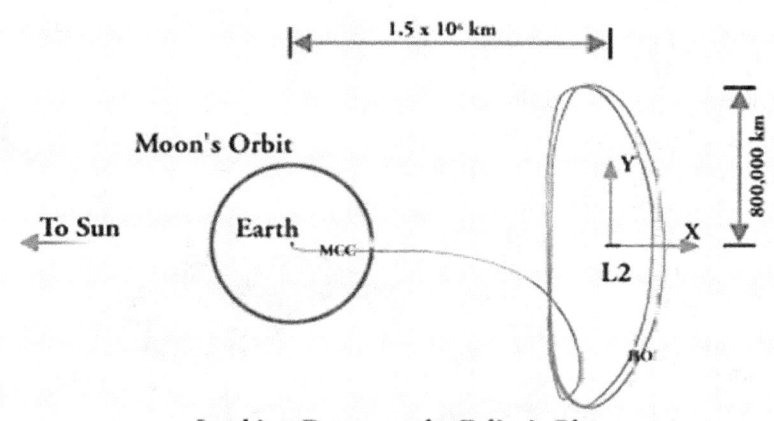

Looking Down on the Ecliptic Plane

STScI

The relay satellite will be parked in a halo orbit around the Earth-Moon L2 Lagrange point. The diagram view is of the ecliptic plane, the plane defined by Earth's orbit about the Sun. In a two-body gravitational system such as the Earth-Moon system, there are five points in space in which a small satellite can be parked with stability or near-stability. These are called Lagrange points or libration points. It is possible to put a satellite in "orbit" around the near-stable points (Lagrange points 1, 2, and 3), even though there is no mass at the Lagrange point. These are called "halo orbits." The satellite's trajectory is not a true orbit around the Lagrange point, but is best described a periodic trajectory around it. The Lagrange point (and the halo orbit) move with the Moon. The diagram shows the trajectory of the satellite from the time of its launch from Earth (line in black, then red).

wind—a magnetized plasma consisting primarily of protons and electrons.

China will send a relay satellite to orbit the Moon, enabling communication with the lander and rover from mission control, and for sending data back to Earth. The relay satellite will be launched from Earth orbit into a lunar transfer orbit first, followed by the lander and rover. The relay satellite will enter a halo orbit around the Earth-Moon L2 Lagrange point (see **Figure 1**), located about 37,000 miles (60,000 km) beyond the Moon. This is considered the best location for a near-stationary communications satellite covering the Moon's far side, while the line of sight to Earth for radiowave communication is never blocked by the Moon. The satellite is expected to be operational for three years.

International Support for Chang'e-4

While the usual suspects in Washington are unnerved by the prospects of "Communist" China making such progress, the U.S. and international scientific community is extremely excited. One of the largest known impact craters in the Solar System, the Moon's South-Pole Aitken Basin, may feature exposed mantle materials, according to Clive Neal of the Lunar Exploration Analysis Group affiliated with NASA. "There has been no surface exploration of the far side," Neal told Agence France Presse. "I am sure the international lunar science community will be very excited about this mission. I know I am."

In 2015, China sent out invitations internationally to institutions that might wish to take advantage of this mission by making proposals for experiments to be carried out on the

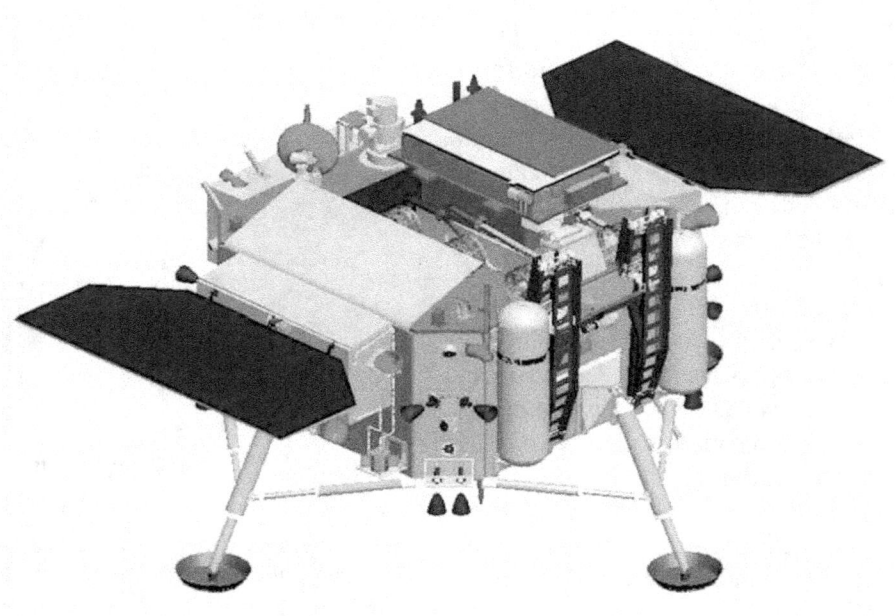

The Chang'e-4 lander concept as of June 2015.

lunar far side. While China's space program began, as did the U.S. and Soviet programs, as primarily a military venture, it has been placed in a civilian agency. The China National Space Administration has expressed great interest in cooperating with other space agencies, and many agencies have shown a great deal of interest in such cooperation. The only outlier is the United States, where legislation passed by Congress has placed draconian restrictions on cooperation with China in space. In many respects, the Chinese program has replaced the role the U.S. program traditionally played, in encouraging space activities in all the countries of the world. For the Chang'e-4 mission, China has invited private enterprises to take part, and is conducting a competition to fly a small scientific instrument on the orbiter or lander, which will undoubtedly engage the interest of students.

China-Russia Collaboration

The success of the Chinese space program has been greatly assisted by Russia, its great neighbor to the north, which inherited the bulk of the Soviet space program. And as the Chang'e-4 mission shows, their cooperation continues. While Russia is rebuilding much of the capabilities destroyed during the Yeltsin period, it is continually under fire from the United

States and its British friends, intent on "keeping Russia down."

But Russia's collaboration with China has been mutually beneficial, with Russia contributing its expertise in space and China prepared to invest in the development of the Russian Far East. The close relationship between China and Russia has also served to help China assume its rightful role in the world, even in an environment in which China is still seen by the West as a potentially hostile power. Chinese efforts to counter this impression are coming up against decades of Cold War propaganda, which have left its traces in the fears and antagonisms of the Western population, propaganda which is being consciously revived to serve the war-mongering stance of the Obama Administration.

The U.S. "color revolution" in Ukraine and the "pivot" to Asia have together soured the relationships between these two important nations—Russia and China—and the United States, and have placed them both on a war footing.

Nevertheless, China has continued to progress and has very successfully mobilized its neighbors and the world to participate in President Xi Jinping's "Belt and Road," a program of infrastructure investment that promises to transform the region into a transmission

President John F. Kennedy visits a NASA launch site.

belt of industrial and agricultural production and cooperation between East and West.

A Stark Choice for the West

At the same time, when viewing the condition of the Western economies, one is reminded of Edward Gibbon's *Decline and Fall of the Roman Empire*. The U.S. economy has become a veritable rust belt, and that includes our transportation system and overall infrastructure.

The submission to Wall Street's demands that "shareholder prices" be maintained at the cost of productive investments, including infrastructure, has driven the living standards of what were considered middle class families into bankruptcy and even homelessness. As a result, the suicide rate is increasing expo-

nentially. And our failure to continue a "war on drugs" has condemned an ever-increasing proportion of our youth population to a lifelong addiction and, in many instances, to an early grave.

The wars of the Bush and Obama administrations have created a flood of refugees from the war-torn Middle East into a Europe already savaged by murderous austerity administered by that satrapy of the London banking system, the European Union.

The direction that the Obama Administration and the European powers have taken by meekly submitting to the dictates of a bankrupt financial system—rather than taking measures to protect the people from the depredations of an out-of-control financial oligarchy through an immediate return to the Glass-Steagall firewall—has condemned the populations of these countries to an early death, perhaps even through the nuclear holocaust that the oligarchs are intent on provoking.

It doesn't have to be that way. The alternative has been laid out by China, Russia, and India in the Silk Road Economic Belt, the Twenty-first Century Maritime Silk Road, and the program of space exploration. We can depart from the dangerous game of geopolitics and join in a win-win effort to begin to rebuild the world's crumbling physical economy.

As economist and statesman Lyndon LaRouche noted in conversations with colleagues on February 1: "Now if you look at the picture of a map of society, you will say that most of the society we talk about, the trans-Atlantic community is a failure. It has been a failure. As of now, it continues to be a failure. And we are trying to kick it back into some kind of effectiveness. But, the fact is, we need to depend on the leading role of Russia and China. Now Russia and China are a different part of the whole planet than the other parts in general. India is part of this group of interest."

What China has launched in Asia could become the path for moving humanity away from the imminent war danger and toward the "new frontier" of space, of which President Kennedy was an early leader, this time not as a space "race," but rather as a collaborative effort of all nations to achieve the common aims of mankind.

The Scientific Importance of China's Lunar Far Side Mission

by Benjamin Deniston

Feb. 2—An edited adaptation of the author's presentation as part of the LaRouche PAC Webcast of Feb. 5, 2016.

The clearest counterpoint to Obama shutting down and destroying our space-faring capabilities is China—over the same time period—establishing itself as one of the leading nations in space exploration. China is clearly vectored towards becoming the number one nation in space exploration, given the current trajectories: The United States has been heading down; China is on a rapid path upwards. In the last few years, this reality grabbed the attention of the world with a key breakthrough in China's lunar exploration program. In December 2013, China made the first soft landing of a rover on the Moon in decades—since the mid-1970s—with its Chang'e-3 mission, deploying the Yutu rover as part of the mission. This captured the attention—and the imagination—of the world.

China's Lunar Exploration Program

Deployment of the Yutu rover was just one part of China's lunar exploration program, the Chang'e program, which has three phases: The first phase, now complete, was to put orbiters around the Moon and investigate it from orbit. The second phase, now ongoing, uses landers and rovers, including the brilliant success of the 2013 Chang'e-3 mission and its Yutu rover (see **Figure 1**). China has just released more high-resolution images of this mission.[1]

---

1. Available on a website of the National Astronomical Observatories of the Chinese Academy of Sciences titled "Science and Application

FIGURE 1

1st Chang'e-3 Color Panorama   Mosaic Credit: CNSA/Chinanews/Ken Kremer/Marco Di Lorenzo

CNSA/Chinanews/Ken Kremer/Marco Di Lorenzo

A segment of the first 360-degree color panorama taken by the Chang'e-3 lander, showing the rover after its disembarkation from the lander. The Chang'e-3 rover is the first to travel on the Moon's surface in 40 years. Exciting video of the Dec. 16, 2013 disembarkation is published here by On Demand News.

FIGURE 2

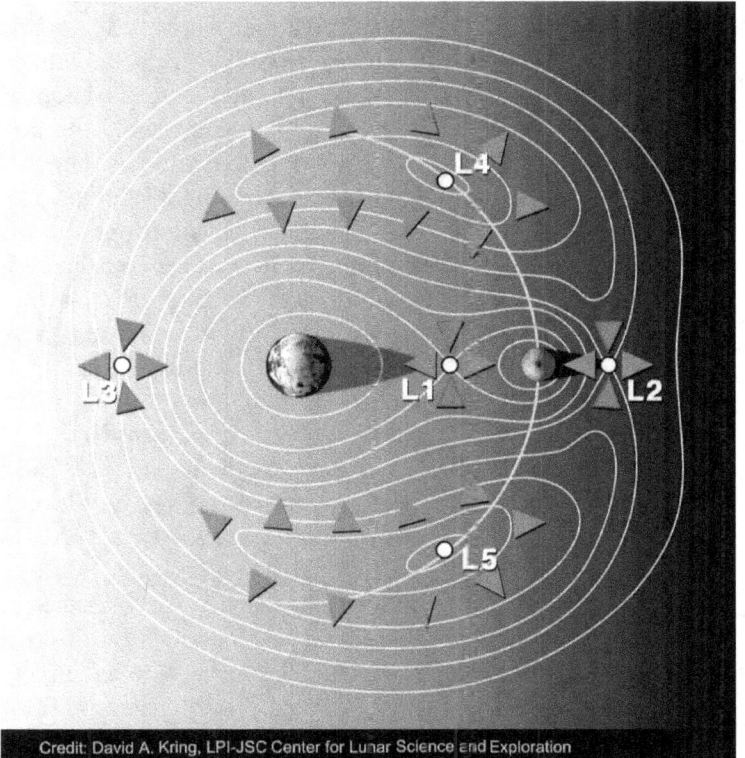

Credit: David A. Kring, LPI-JSC Center for Lunar Science and Exploration

David A. Kring, LPI-JSC Center for Lunar Science and Exploration

The five stable and near-stable locations created by the gravitational interaction of the Earth and the Moon, called Lagrange points or L-points, after the Italian mathematician and astronomer Joseph-Louis Lagrange (Giuseppe Lodovico Lagrangia) who first defined them. He died in 1813, long before the first spaceflight. The Chang'e-4 relay satellite will be parked at L2. The contour lines represent gravitational field strength and show why the L-points are where they are.

The Chang'e-4 mission is part of this second, landing-and-rover phase. It was initially reserved as a backup, in case something went wrong with Chang'e-3. Since Chang'e-3 was a success, it wasn't needed as a backup. Now it has been announced that Chang'e-4 has a new objective, *landing on the far side of the Moon.* That will conclude the second phase. The third phase involves landing, acquiring a sample from the lunar surface, and returning it to Earth.

Initially the Chang'e-4 lunar far side landing was planned for 2020; now the National Space Administration has announced it for late 2018. So China has also accelerated the timeframe. It will be the first time ever that mankind has landed anything on the far side of the Moon. All of the Apollo missions were to the near side;

Center for Moon and Deepspace Exploration." Exciting video of the rover's disembarkation is here.

all of the Soviet unmanned missions were to the near side. We have sent orbiters around the Moon that have imaged the far side, imaged all of the Moon. But this will be the first time that mankind has ever landed any device on the far side.

Sometimes the far side is referred to as the "dark side" of the Moon. It is not really so. In every 28-day orbit of the Moon around Earth, the Moon will show both its face and its far side to the Sun, so the far side is dark only part of the time. You *could* say "dark side" in reference to mankind's knowledge of it, which is a fair expression, because it is always facing away from us. However, this does create some problems.

The difficulty is that the far side is in a state of constant radio blackout with respect to communications with Earth, because the mass of the Moon is always between the far side and the Earth. So part of this Chang'e-4 mission is to send a relay satellite out to what's called the Earth-Moon L2 point, an interesting, stable position in the gravitational interaction between the Earth and the Moon. The L2 point is one of a few "L-points," which are very advantageous for space agencies as parking spots, so to speak, in different orbital locations, where we can park satellites without much drift. For the Chang'e-4 mission, China will use the L2 point, which is beyond the Moon—along a straight line extending from Earth through the Moon, a line that therefore moves with the Moon as it orbits the Earth (see **Figure 2**).

The intention is to send a relay satellite to this L2 location; there, it will always have a line of sight to Earth for communications. And it will always have a line of sight for communications with the Chang'e-4 lander on the lunar far side. With this configuration, China will be positioned to have the first-ever landing on, and direct investigation of the lunar far side. This is a first, a first for mankind.

Why the Far Side?

What's so interesting about the far side of the Moon? This must be considered in light of what Kesha Rogers has recently emphasized as Krafft Ehricke's insightful understanding of the *necessity* for mankind to develop into a species of the Solar System, so to speak. The far side of the Moon offers certain unique and critical points of investigation for mankind.

FIGURE 3

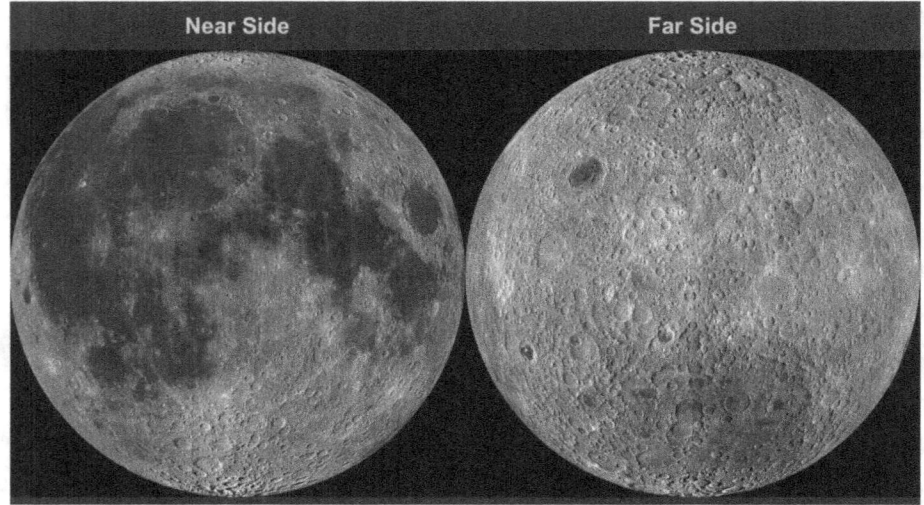

Near Side | Far Side

NASA

The near and far sides of the Moon, imaged by NASA's Lunar Reconnaissance Orbiter launched in 2009. Dramatic, close-up video of features on both sides is found here*.*

FIGURE 4

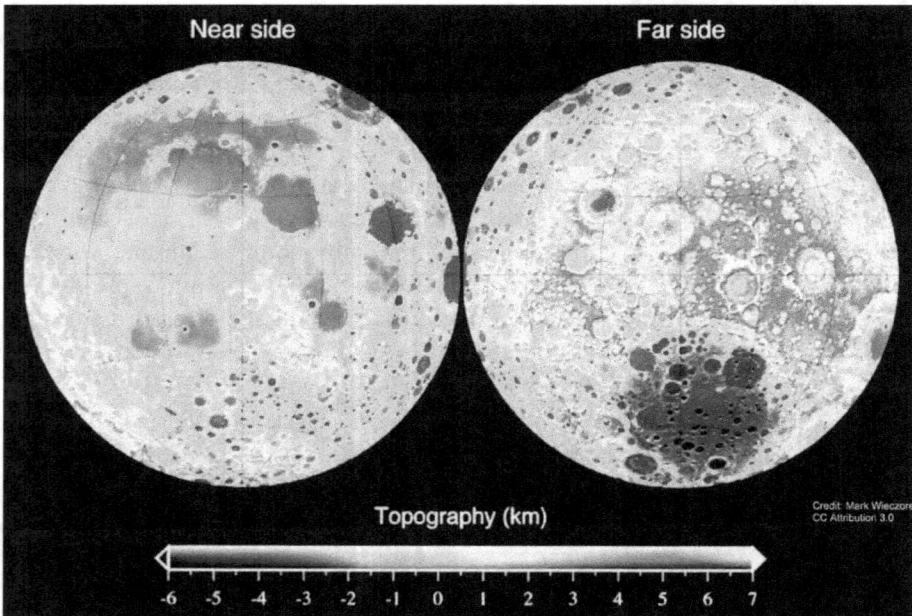

Near side | Far side

Topography (km)

Credit: Mark Wieczorek
CC Attribution 3.0

-6 -5 -4 -3 -2 -1 0 1 2 3 4 5 6 7

Mark Wieczorek; CC Attribution 3.0

A topographical (elevation) map of the Moon. The deep purple near the South Pole on the far side is the Aitken Basin, about six kilometers deep and 2,500 kilometers in diameter.

For example, the far side may have a higher concentration of helium-3, which we've discussed.[2] It is thought that because the near side is often shielded from the Sun by the Earth, the Earth has blocked some of the deposition of helium-3 by the solar wind on the lunar near side. The far side, always facing away from Earth, is thought to have a higher concentration of this helium-3, probably the best fusion fuel known to us. The Sun has been creating this unique isotope and pumping it out into the Solar System. It has been embedding itself on the lunar surface for a few billion years, so you've got quite a build-up there.

Geophysical Anomalies

Second, the lunar far side also has a unique geology. In the high resolution images from NASA's Lunar Reconnaissance Orbiter you can clearly see that the far side has a dramatically different look. The near side is largely covered by dark patches; these *maria*[3] were produced by volcanic flows. The far side has less of that, making it a more direct representation of the earlier stages of the Moon, less affected by the volcanic activity which occurred later. So, if we want to answer some basic questions about the Moon, its formation, its interaction with the Solar System, and even the interaction of the Solar System with the galaxy—looking for places where we can get long, deep records about what experiences different parts of planets have had over the past billions of years—this is really crucial stuff. And there are other interesting features you can see on the far side.

If we examine the Moon's topographical characteristics, one of the places of great interest is the Aitken Basin, a very large, deep impact crater near the South Pole on the far side (see **Figure 4**). China may decide

---

2. See the material on the LaRouche PAC page, "The Lunar Helium-3 Fusion Driver."

3. The plural of Latin *mare* (sea). Formerly, astronomers thought these volcanic plains were actually seas.

to bring its Chang'e-4 lander down here. It is of great geological interest because it is one of the largest known impact craters in the Solar System: it is so deep (about 6 km) that it reaches into some lower layers of the lunar surface, making them accessible for investigation.

Some people might think, "Lunar geology, how interesting can that be? This is just a giant, cold, dead rock up there; how much can you learn from that?" But we are constantly being humbled by our realization of how little we know about the Solar System, about planetary bodies. When the Apollo astronauts went to the Moon, they brought seismometers to measure seismic activity. They thought they might measure seismic activity from thermal expansion due to differential solar heating of the Moon, and seismic activity from meteorite impacts. They measured those phenomena, but they also measured deep, earthquake-like seismic activity in the Moon (moonquakes), something they didn't think could happen. They didn't expect it; we still don't really have an explanation for why the Moon is still seismically active.

Radio Astronomy at Very Low Frequencies

The following scientific areas are among those identified as potentially benefitting from very low frequency radio observations of the universe.[1]

The unexpected unknown. First and foremost: *things we don't know and can't foresee!* Every time we open up a new window on the universe, we find things we didn't expect. This is perhaps the most important potential of the entire effort.

Magnetic fields. Magnetic fields can be hard to detect and measure from afar, but because they are often associated with plasma structures, and because plasma structures radiate at very low frequencies, some new investigations of magnetic fields on various scales may become possible.

Large-scale plasma structures. On planetary, stellar, interstellar, and galactic scales, there are large, coherent plasma structures that can be investigated because they radiate in very low frequencies.

Solar activity. We may obtain a new picture of solar activity, potentially shedding light on the nature of the energetic, explosive events underlying solar flares and coronal mass ejections—processes that are not currently fully understood.

Planetary imaging. Images of the radio activity (including that resulting from lightning) of the outer planets—Jupiter, Saturn, Uranus, and Neptune. Some very limited, low-frequency radio measurements were done by the Voyager spacecraft decades ago, but there is much to learn.

Asteroid and comet detection. Observations at very low frequencies may provide a new way to detect asteroids and comets. As they travel through the interplanetary medium, asteroids and comets excite the solar wind (a plasma), causing it to radiate in these very low frequencies.[2]

Low-energy cosmic rays. Cosmic rays below a certain energy cannot penetrate the Sun's heliosphere, so we currently know nothing about them, but they can radiate in very low frequencies.

Supernovae remnants. Certain parts of supernovae remnants are expected to radiate in the very low frequencies.

Structure of the Milky Way Galaxy. Certain features of the Galaxy's magnetic fields and the interstellar medium can be investigated.

Radio galaxies and other active galaxies. The mysterious phenomena of active galactic nuclei can be illuminated in a completely new way, which may shed some light on one of the most interesting mysteries of galactic astronomy.

---

1. Unless otherwise noted, these are some scientific potentials summarized in the 1997 ESA report, "Very Low Frequency Array On The Lunar Far Side."

2. Proposed at the 1992 Los Alamos National Laboratory planetary defense conference. See "Space Optical and Low-Frequency Radio Searches for Earth-Crossing Asteroids and Comets" by J. G. Hills in *Proceedings of the Near-Earth Object Interception Workshop*, LANL, Los Alamos, New Mexico, Jan. 14-16, 1992.

Or take a more recent discovery. Just in the last couple of years, we've found evidence that the Moon was still volcanically active within the last 100 million years. Earlier, experts had thought it hadn't been volcanically active for billions of years; they thought it was just a cold, dead body up there. Now, speaking in terms of geological time scales, we find that it has been volcanically active in the relatively recent past.[4]

Not only that, but these recent periods of lunar volcanic activity correspond to times when the Earth has experienced very intense volcanic activity.[5] Is that a coincidence? Maybe. Is it an indication of some process on a larger scale, affecting the Solar System as a whole? It could be.

These kinds of things direct our attention to the larger system of the galaxy.[6] It's amazing how little we know about the fundamentals of the Solar System, of planetary bodies. So it is crucial to get up there and actually investigate.

The (Radio) Dark Side

Third, the lunar far side offers an entirely new window for our investigation of the universe as a whole: It will enable us to observe cosmic phenomena in the very low frequency part of the radio spectrum for the first time. Very low frequency radio astronomy from the

4. S.E. Braden et al., "Evidence for Basaltic Volcanism on the Moon within the Past 100 Million Years," *Nature Geoscience* 7, 787-791. Published online Oct. 12, 2014.
5. See Benjamin Deniston, "Earth-Moon Comparative Planetology," *EIR*, July 17, 2015; and Benjamin Deniston, "Near Simultaneous Multi-Planet Volcanism on Geological Timescales as Evidence for a Cosmic Driver of Planetary Geophysical Activity?" *New Concepts in Global Tectonics*, 4:1 (March 2016), in press.
6. See "Toward a Galactic Science Driver," Benjamin Deniston, *EIR*, July 17, 2015.

FIGURE 5

GSFC Scientific Visualization Studio, SDO, NASA

Different frequencies of the electromagnetic spectrum disclose different phenomena. This is a montage of the Sun imaged at different frequencies, some showing the solar "granulation," some disclosing magnetic field organization, and others showing flare activity. The electromagnetic spectrum extends from gamma rays (high frequency) through X-rays, ultraviolet, visible light (violet to red), infrared, microwaves, and radio waves (low frequency).

far side is under consideration as a part of the new Chang'e-4 mission.

Why is this important? We don't observe the universe just in one part of the electromagnetic spectrum. Our eyes enable us to see light from the red to the violet, which we call the visible range of the spectrum. But we know that this is just a tiny fraction of the entire spectrum in which processes in the universe radiate. As we have discovered more and more of the electromagnetic spectrum, we have also developed instruments to detect and image phenomena in the universe at those wavelengths. And we have been surprised every time we have done it, finding things we didn't expect.

The image of the Sun in **Figure 5** illustrates the point. It is a montage of images taken at the same time, but with a variety of instruments, each sensitive to a different window of the electromagnetic spectrum, giving a sense of what different processes we see when we look in the different parts of the spectrum.

The same principle can be impressively demonstrated when looking at galaxies. If we look in the optical—what we're used to seeing with backyard tele-

FIGURE 6

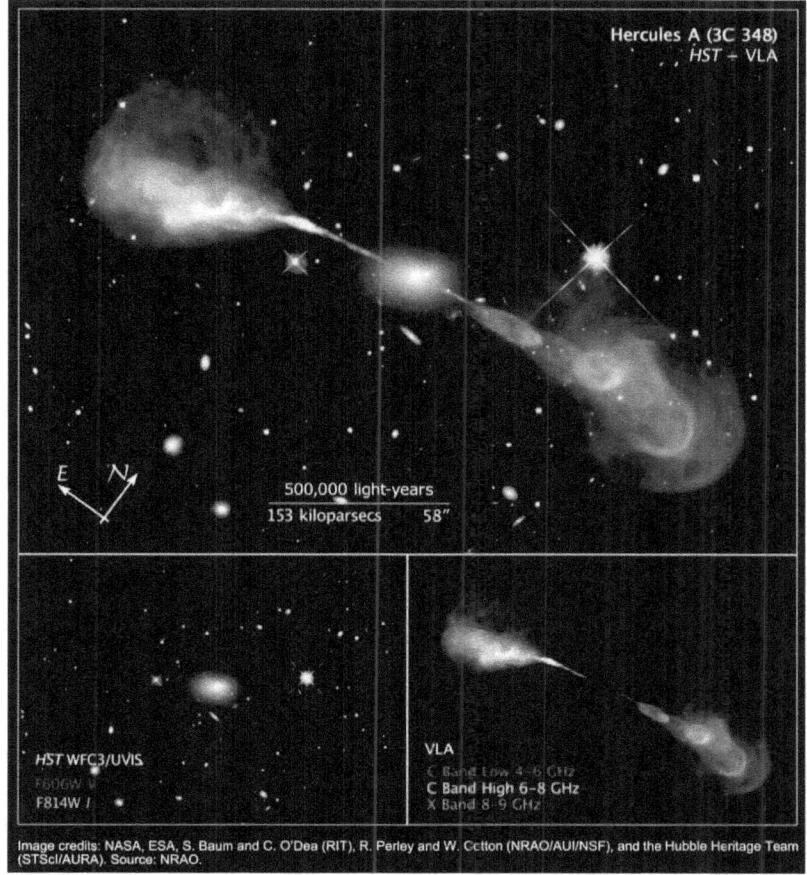

Image credits: NASA, ESA, S. Baum and C. O'Dea (RIT), R. Perley and W. Cotton (NRAO/AUI/NSF), and the Hubble Heritage Team (STScI/AURA). Source: NRAO.

NASA, ESA, S. Baum and C. O'Dea (RIT), R. Perley and W. Cotton (NRAO/AUI/NSF), and the Hubble Heritage Team (STScI/AURA). Source: NRAO

The Hercules A galaxy in radio and optical wavelengths. Lower left, the galaxy as captured by the Hubble Space Telescope in visible and ultraviolet light, showing galaxies but no plasma jets. Lower right, the same location captured in radio waves with the Very Large Array, showing plasma jets but no galaxy. Above, the two images are combined.

scopes, and the Hubble Space Telescope has an optical capability—we might see a spiral disk, or the form of an elliptical galaxy. If we look using radio frequencies, at the known locations of certain galaxies we see something completely different, something we would otherwise never know was there. Sometimes you see massive structures of plasma in the radio part of the spectrum. So an entire, critical phenomenon, central to what is going on in the fundamental physical properties of these galactic systems, is completely invisible in the optical. It's only when we look in certain other wavelengths that we get a completely new window (see **Figure 6**).

Mankind has been doing this for decades. We have been putting up satellites to look in more intense energy ranges, that is, using higher frequencies—in the ultraviolet, the X-ray, and the gamma ray. We have also been going in the other direction, using infrared and longer wavelengths, that is, at lower energies, down into the radio range. And there is still a lot to be done; we're constantly looking with higher resolution, we're looking farther, we're getting clearer pictures

But there is one large chunk of the spectrum that we have not utilized in looking into the universe, we have never been able to image the universe in very low frequency radio waves,[7] that is, very long wavelength radio waves. We have never done it because we cannot do it from the Earth. Many of the longer radio wavelength ranges simply do not penetrate to Earth's surface; they bounce off of the ionosphere structure of the atmosphere. We also use long radio wavelengths massively for communications, so the Earth environment is very noisy in these regions. And the Earth itself emits very strong signals in these regions. For these reasons, even Earth-orbiting satellites can't do the job. It is impossible from Earth, even from Earth orbit, to observe the universe in this entire low-frequency range of the spectrum in a fruitful way.

For decades, scientists have realized that the perfect location for making such observations is the far side of the Moon.[8] Being the far side, always facing away from the Earth, it is always shielded from all the radio noise from the Earth (natural and manmade) by the mass of the Moon itself. The Moon has an incredibly thin atmosphere, so the very low frequency signals from the universe can penetrate down to the lunar surface. So we have a unique window from the Moon to begin looking at the universe in a completely new part of the spectrum.

_____

7. For the astronomers, very low frequency (VLF) refers to a low of a few hundred kilohertz to a high in the tens of megahertz. This differs from the definition of very low frequency used by the electrical engineer, which is significantly lower.
8. In the United States, the 2007 National Research Council report on the general scientific importance of returning to the Moon (*The Scientific Context for Exploration of the Moon*) emphasizes the unique importance of lunar far side very low frequency astronomy (Section 6).

It has been discussed since the 1960s;[9] it has been studied in detail by numerous teams in terms of the importance of accessing this part of the spectrum and of demonstrating that the Moon's far side is really the only nearby place we are going to be able to do this.[10]

There is some discussion about what we might find by using this region of the spectrum. In the very large, certain fundamental processes of galaxies are thought to radiate only in this region. On the smaller scale of our Solar System, some basic processes of our Sun are thought to only radiate in this region (see box, p. 13). For example, we still don't know why there are explosive events on the surface of the Sun—the solar flares and coronal mass ejections—which pose a threat to our astronauts out in space and to our satellite grid and electrical systems. We still don't understand the basic physics of how these explosive solar events occur, and this part of the spectrum has been posited as crucial to

---

9. As discussed in Section 2.1 of *New Astronomy from the Moon: A Lunar Based Very Low Frequency Radio Array* by Yuki David Takahashi (2003).

10. In 1997—following multiple, in-depth studies—a 70-page European Space Agency report was dedicated to the subject, "Very Low Frequency Array on The Lunar Far Side."

understanding it.

But on all scales—and perhaps most importantly—beyond what we think we might find, there is also what we don't think we might find—the unknown unknowns, waiting to be discovered.

Some very preliminary test observations in this low-frequency window are being proposed as a possible part of the Chang'e-4 far side mission. It could mean the opening up of an entire new window on the universe, showing us new features and processes in the activity of our Sun, our Solar System, our Galaxy, and in the galaxies beyond.

The proposal for such observations and the Chang'e program more broadly stand in critical contrast to what Kesha Rogers has emphasized about the course the United States is taking. China is taking clear, decisive steps, establishing itself as a world leader in space exploration, and now positioning itself to take fundamental first steps into new domains that mankind has never entered before. That is the direction that mankind should be taking; that is the direction China is going in. And you contrast that with where we have gone under Obama, in the exact same period, and I think you get a very clear picture of what the challenge is.

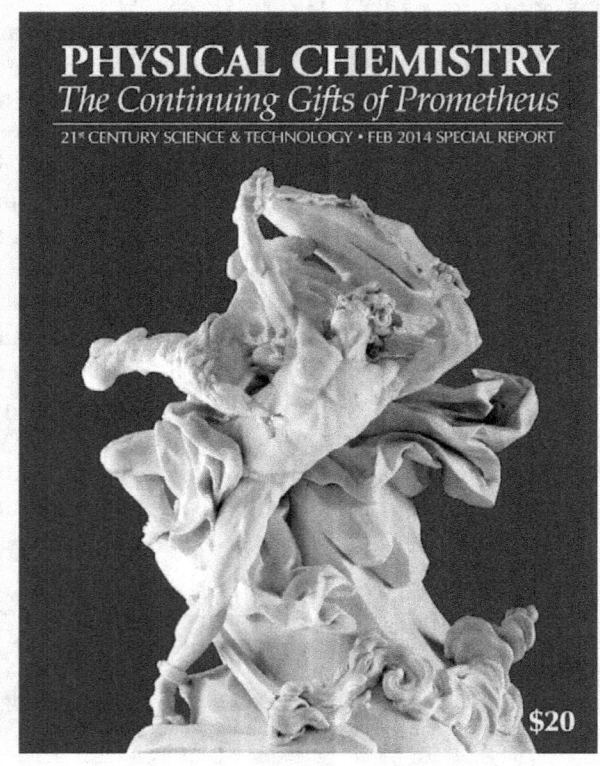

How America's Space Program Has Been Nearly Destroyed

by Marsha Freeman

Feb. 6—Virtually within minutes of President Kennedy's announcement, on May 25, 1961, that this nation would commit itself, before the end of the decade, "to land a man on the Moon and return him safely to the Earth," London-based think tanks and their American co-conspirators were plotting how to destroy the Apollo program. These masters of geopolitics, who controlled an empire on which the Sun never set through psychological, as well as military warfare, could see the potential danger to their future, of such a thrust into space.

Setting mankind on the path to take responsibility for discovering and developing what lay beyond our planet, would not only create a quantum leap in science, and lay the basis for successive technological revolutions, but would create a cultural paradigm shift, restoring the United States to a position of true leadership, based on creating the future to fulfill the "common aims of mankind." An America that returned to the moral imperative of its Constitution would be an inspiration to the subjugated nations of the third world, and help give impetus to their drive to free themselves from the yoke of empire, support for which was, in fact, a hallmark of President

President Kennedy announcing, on Sept. 12, 1962 at Rice University in Texas, that because of scientific progress the exploration of space was inevitable, and that the U.S.A. should begin "before this decade is out," to inspire and engage the nation.

NASA

Kennedy's short time in the White House.

This potential of the space program to reshape human history for the future, was recognized at the time by only a handful of visionaries. Among them were the German space pioneers, who had an outlook informed by the German classics and the philosophical outlook of the Renaissance. And leaders such as NASA Administrator James Webb, who represented the American Hamiltonian economic tradition, then most recently expressed by former President Franklin Delano Roosevelt. To them, the "space program" was not a collection of separate, seemingly unconnected missions, but as German-American space pioneer Krafft Ehricke would explain, an "extraterrestrial imperative." Exploring space is an expression of the very essence of mankind's creativity, which ennobles humanity. It is imperative, because the alternative belief, that there is a limit to man's creative capabilities, and therefore limits to growth, denies mankind's ability to create his future, and is ultimately, as we see today, a death sentence.

The goals of the space program, which require decades to carry out and substantial resources to be met, depend upon leadership from the White House. It is, therefore, indicative of the quality of the presidencies since John F. Kennedy, that there has been no visionary space program carried out since Apollo.

The Apollo 'Dead End'

As NASA's budget was steadily increased into the mid-1960s to carry out the mission of President Kennedy's Apollo program, and then the landing on the Moon became a reality, intense attacks on the space program gained momentum. This assault was originated and led by institutions of the British Empire from London. It was designed to appeal to every possible constituency, in order to marshal enough "public" opposition to cripple the program. The publication of London's Tavistock Institute, *Human Relations,* proposed that the space program was producing "redundant" and "supernumerary" scientists and engineers. "There would soon be two scientists for every man, woman, and dog in the society," one report warned. Others complained that the space program was absorbing so much of the nation's technical manpower, there would be shortages in other fields of science.

"Liberal" think tanks, such as the Brookings Institution, proposed that the space agency be concerned with the impact of its activity on society. Brookings charged that the money "spent in space" (sic) would "require vast investments of men, and materials, and creative effort—investments which could be profitably applied also to other areas of human endeavor," such as the alleviation of poverty. A series of "sociological" studies of the space program, foisted upon NASA in the 1960s, likewise warned of the negative "social consequences" of the Apollo program.

The "religious right" was mobilized, to object to this intrusion by man "into God's firmament." This argument was eloquently countered by Pope Paul VI, who stated that all of God's creation was under man's dominion, and he blessed the Apollo astronauts before their journey, watched Neil Armstrong's first step live on television, and met with the Apollo 11 crew upon their return.

While President Kennedy was alive, and through the presidency of Lyndon Johnson, who was committed to accomplishing the goal the martyred President had set, these frontal assaults on the Apollo program and the psyche of the American public gained limited traction, as Americans, and people around the world, watched in excitement and anticipation, as mankind took his first steps off planet Earth. But the seeds had been planted.

By the time Neil Armstrong took the first step on to the Moon, in July 1969, the effort was well underway to undermine the optimism and future-orientation of space exploration, and place in its stead the mind-deadening rock-drug counterculture and the Malthusian zero-growth, anti-science outlook, which was exactly what Krafft Ehricke had warned against.

The Dionysian drug-laced Woodstock Festival took place only three weeks after the Moon landing, and in March of the next year the first Earth Day celebrations were held, unleashing a wave of mass recruitment into the anti-science anti-human environmentalist movement of Britain's Prince Philip.

But the legacy of the Apollo program is still evident today, most notably in the leaders of numerous space missions, many of whom as youngsters were inspired by the lunar landings, to study science and engineering and dedicate their careers to exploration. In recent years, there has been a relentless drive to erase from memory the inspiration of President Kennedy and Apollo. Myths about the Apollo program were created, in a rewriting of history, in order to steal from humanity the pride of what mankind had accomplished and the hope that such a mobilization could be launched in the future.

It is often stated, that the Apollo paradigm should not be repeated, because the program was a failure, a "dead end." Not in President Kennedy's mind! In his announcement of the lunar landing program, the President included "an additional $23 million to accelerate the development of the Rover nuclear rocket. This gives the promise of someday providing a means for even more exciting and ambitious exploration of space, perhaps beyond the Moon, perhaps to the very end of the Solar System itself." The Apollo program was to be just the beginning.

One reads in history books that there was no bold follow-on to Apollo because the American public "lost interest" in space. This assertion is also not true. It is estimated that one million people came to Cape Canaveral on July 29, 1969, to watch the Apollo 11 crew launch to the Moon. An estimated 600 million people around the world watched it live on TV. After the astronauts returned, their "Giantstep Apollo-11" tour took them to 24 countries, where they were enthusiastically greeted by thousands of citizens at each stop. In the view of most of the population, the Space Age was just getting underway.

Even before the Apollo 11 mission, at a time when much of the hardware for the lunar landing was under development, NASA Administrator Webb had stressed to the Johnson Administration and to the Congress that post-Apollo manned space programs had to be decided upon, authorized, and begun immediately. If not, he warned, the capabilities the nation had created would be dismantled.

Although personally committed to the Apollo legacy of JFK, Lyndon Johnson and his presidency lived in the shadow of the assassin's rifle. President Johnson once told a close associate that the "cross-hairs" of a rifle scope were on his neck. Under pressure from London and Wall Street, Johnson plunged the nation into the Vietnam War, draining billions of dollars from the economy and turning millions of Americans, particularly young Americans, against their own government. These developments, all engineered by the oligarchical interests who had murdered John F. Kennedy, combined with the financial costs of his effort to alleviate poverty through his "Great Society" programs, led President Lyndon Johnson, once President Kennedy's greatest supporter for an aggressive space program, to propose cuts to NASA's budget. The peak funding year for NASA was actually 1965, four years prior to the Moon landing.

By 1969 Richard Nixon was in the White House, and the thousands of young American boys were being shipped home from Vietnam in body bags. The optimism of 1961 was being replaced by the disillusionment and cynicism of 1969. The American people increasingly mistrusted their own government, a government which had covered up President Kennedy's assassination.

As the optimism of the Kennedy years disappeared, helped by a well-funded campaign and media barrage, planning for mankind's future in the Solar System was overwhelmed and nearly buried in the calls for "limits to growth," the "protection" of the environment at the expense of economic development, and the proposition that the age of progress was over.

The Failure of Austerity Economics

Another myth that has been promulgated to "explain" the multiple near-deaths of the space program, is that NASA did not know what to do next, after it had attained the goal set by President Kennedy. This assertion also was not true.

The drug-laced Woodstock Festival, three weeks after the Moon landing, unleashed a wave of mass recruitment into the anti-science, anti-human environmentalist movement of Britain's Prince Philip.

Months before the lunar landing, President Nixon had established a Space Task Group, headed by Vice President Spiro Agnew, to develop policy recommendations for NASA's programs through the 1970s. Two months after the landing, in September 1969, the Task Group's report was presented to the President, based on German space pioneer, Wernher von Braun's "Integrated Space Program, 1970-1990." The outline included an Earth-orbital space station, an extended Apollo program that would culminate in a lunar surface base, a family of new transportation systems for deep-space exploration, and, by 1985, a temporary base on the surface of Mars.

The fight within the Nixon Administration over the future of the space program was intense and continued for years. What ultimately determined the outcome, however, was not anything that had to do with the merits of space exploration. Rather, the failure to continue an aggressive "space program" was a result of Richard Nixon's slavish servitude to the interests of London and Wall Street finance.

In 1968 the British government decoupled the British pound from silver, leading to the destruction of the post-war system of fixed exchange rates that had enabled dramatic economic growth since 1945. This British move provoked enormous instability in the global economy and finally led, on August 15, 1971, to the announcement of radical economic austerity measures by the Nixon White House. The setting of wage and price controls, and taking the dollar off the gold reserve standard were, in fact, what would ultimately decide the fate of a far-sighted civilian space program.

Some advisors to the President lobbied for continuing just the planetary and space science missions, and that, at a reduced level. Many voices advised President Nixon that the expense of the manned programs was unsustainable in the economic crisis the country faced, and was a luxury the country could not afford.

After many months, stretching into years, of wavering, President Nixon finally decided that he did not want ending manned space exploration to be part of his legacy. So on Jan. 5, 1971 he announced that the United States would build a reusable Space Transportation System, or shuttle, that would take men and materiel back and forth to low-Earth orbit. Completely missing from Nixon's proposal were the space station, (the destination for the Shuttle, in von Braun's plan), the follow-on development of the Moon, and the robotic and then manned missions to Mars. They were gone.

Over the succeeding years of the Ford and Carter administrations, presidential programs for space exploration were characterized by a lack of vision, or failed economic policies, and sometimes, both.

On Jan. 28, 1986, seventy three seconds after lift-off, the Space Shuttle Challenger exploded with seven astronauts on board and in full sight of the visitors at Cape Canaveral, including the students who were there to cheer on Christa McAuliffe, the first Teacher in Space. President Ronald Reagan cancelled that night's scheduled State of the Union address to speak to a nation that was in shock and mourning. At 5 PM, from the Oval Office, the President said: "We'll continue our quest. There will be more shuttle flights and more shuttle crews.... Nothing ends here; our hopes and our journeys continue."

President Reagan lived up to his promise, and took the unprecedented step of allocating more than $1 billion to NASA to replace the Challenger with a new orbiter, later named Endeavor. In his 1984 State of the Union address, the President had also instructed NASA to build an orbiting space station within a decade. With a replacement Shuttle orbiter, and the start of a space station program, it appeared NASA had been given the go-ahead for the next step.

There is no question of President Reagan's intention to continue the exploration of space. Reagan's commitment to a Renaissance for frontier work in science and space exploration had already been signaled through his collaboration with Lyndon LaRouche in the initiation of the Strategic Defense Initiative.

Unfortunately, after the attempted assassination of Reagan in March of 1981, circles associated with Vice President Bush increasingly gained the upper hand in his administration, and polices of brutal economic austerity and free trade became the order of the day. The economic agenda became one of reducing government spending, cutting taxes, and letting the "free market" run the economy, effectively halting any progress in areas of research and development that the President otherwise personally supported, such as advanced nuclear energy technology. It also became impossible to fulfill Reagan's directives for the space program. At one point, the White House even tried, unsuccessfully, to find a private company to buy the Space Shuttle fleet.

This fatal economic flaw would also be characteristic of later space initiatives, which would not be funded in times of economic distress.

Following the 2003 Columbia Space Shuttle accident, President George W. Bush unveiled the Constellation program at NASA headquarters. The outline was to create the launch vehicles and new crew vehicles to return Americans to the Moon, with the long-term goal of missions to Mars. But there was a catch. In order to "save money," the work on Constellation would begin only after the Space Shuttles were retired from service, with the deadline set for 2010 to do that. This meant that, by design, there would be a gap of minimally five years, between the end of the Shuttle program, and the first flight of the new crew vehicle. This meant that tens of thousands of engineers and technicians—some of the most skilled in the country—who kept the Shuttle fleet flying, would be out of a job. And as for all of the subsequent complaining by the Congress about U.S. dependence upon the Russians for transporting our astronauts to the International Space Station, they have known that would be the case since the Constellation program was announced in 2003.

With the Congress focused on creating the image of the Russian "evil empire," and complaining about the money paid to Russia for Soyuz flights, it is rarely mentioned that the actual danger in depending solely upon the Russian Soyuz for astronaut transport is that if there is a problem with the Soyuz, there is no backup, and the station would have to be abandoned.

Following all of the initial media hype surrounding the announcement of the Constellation initiative, in the months that followed, all the way through to the end of his two terms, President Bush never requested the money required to keep the program on track. Unlike President Kennedy, who affirmed his support for Apollo throughout his presidency, President Bush never mentioned the program again, throughout his remaining six years in the White House following his announcement of the Constellation program. Instead, the Bush Administration gave America the wars in Iraq and Afghanistan and the biggest government bail-out of Wall Street speculators in U.S. history.

NASA

Neil Armstrong took the first step on the Moon, July 20, 1969.

There Is Still Time

By the time Barack Obama became President, the Constellation program was behind schedule and seriously over budget as a result of the years of underfunding by the Bush Administration. It was estimated by a review panel convened by President Obama that NASA would need a budget increase of about $3 billion per year to keep the Constellation program on track. But President Obama had no intention of taking that route.

Instead, the White House cancelled the Constellation program outright in 2010, and announced that the "private sector," (with massive financial subsidies from NASA) would provide cargo transport to the space station, and would also develop vehicles to transport station crews. The new NASA Ares rocket to take astronauts to the station was cancelled, as was the Orion crew capsule. The Altair lander that would deliver astronauts on the surface of the Moon was also cancelled, along with the technology needed for a return to the Moon. The Congress rebelled, as did former Apollo astronauts. The government, it was charged, was abdicating its responsibility to continue a space exploration program for the benefit of the future of the nation.

The taffy pull between the White House and Capitol Hill on space policy led to the paralysis of NASA programs, and finally led to a series of compromises, which has left space exploration underfunded and directionless. Under relentless attack for its killing of the manned space program, the Administration invented an Asteroid Redirect Mission, which has no purpose at all, and wastes the precious resources still resident in the space agency and U.S. aerospace industry.

All of this has occurred, as the Obama Administration has demanded billions of dollars for military rearmament and has carried out war provocations against both Russia and China, nations which we should be looking to as partners in space exploration instead.

It is fortunate that no other nation has followed the mis-leadership of the United States in space policy. There is a readily-available opportunity to return our space program to our future. China is carrying out a step-by-step program of exploration of the Moon, which will undoubtedly culminate in manned missions. One aim will be to exploit the Moon's resources, such as the rare isotope, helium-3, needed for fusion power. Russia is readying a series of robotic missions to the Moon, and the European Space Agency, Japan, and India are planning lunar exploration, as well. The United States could readily join, and contribute to these missions.

Under the new financial architecture which has been created in China, and globally through Chinese initiative, the option exists to replace failed and self-destructive trans-Atlantic financial and economic policies that have crippled NASA for decades, with economic policies based on promoting the science drivers, such as space exploration, that will reshape the Earth, and open the cosmos for mankind's future.

Plasma Technologies To Build A Truly Human Society

by Stephan Ossenkopp

Feb. 8—Mankind can make a leap into an entirely new world. Recent breakthroughs in German plasma physics deliver a key to open up that possibility.

The discovery and general use of technologies are activities closely related to the unique creativity of the human soul, a characteristic which separates us, in principle, from the domain of other forms of life, including apes and other highly-developed animals.

In the ever-changing course of human development, there are those critical moments when, aided by the use of technologies, man improves his environment of interaction in a fundamental way; and there are those other times, when he neglects his moral progress and falls into a state of decadence. In these latter instances it is not the technologies which are "dangerous," but the evil projects of those who abuse the power of technology to destroy.

Today we are situated in a particularly momentous time, because the technologies which powerful nations or international alliances are able to put into effect, present us with the choice of either a new and unexplored summit of our development, or of unprecedented suffering and likely self-annihilation. If we abhor the thought of our civilization ending up as a gruesome tragedy, we have to muster our strength of will to make the necessary leap into a happy future.

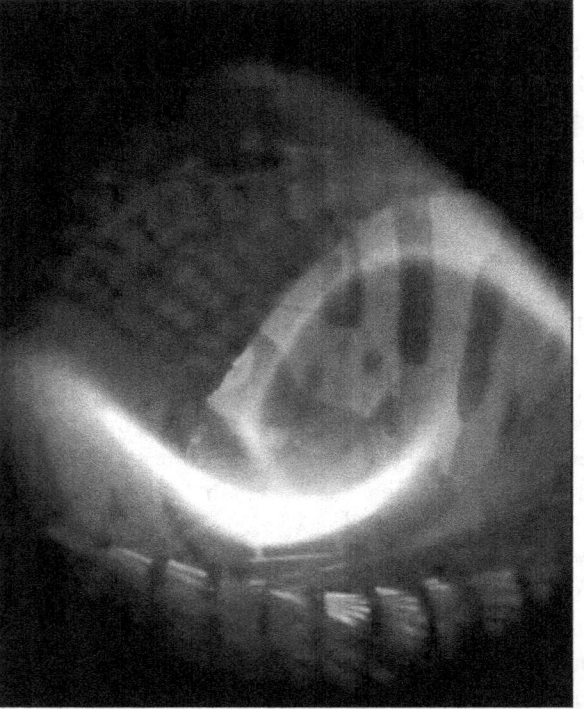

Max Planck Institute for Plasma Physics

The first hydrogen plasma in the Wendelstein 7-X stellarator, the fusion device at Max Planck Institute for Plasma Physics in Greifswald, Germany. This historic event, on Feb. 3, 2016, marked the start of the device's scientific operation. Wendelstein 7-X, the world's largest fusion machine of the stellarator type, will investigate the suitability of the stellarator configuration for use in a power plant.

Technology of the Future

The seed of those technologies with which we are able to create our future and increase our happiness, has already been sown. The general public has just not been adequately informed about the gigantic efforts made by physicists, developers, technicians, and engineers worldwide, to thrust mankind into a new millennium of seemingly boundless opportunities. The German Physical Society has therefore taken steps to showcase some of its most advanced technical equipment to the public.

Not far from Greifswald, a small, beautiful maritime city in northern Germany, lie the extensive facilities of the Max Planck Institute for Plasma Physics, whose staff has worked for roughly ten years to build a one-of-a-kind complex apparatus. They named it simply the Research Facility for High-Temperature Plasma Physics, but it is a unique undertaking, unparalleled in the world, which was realized after intensive international discussions. The aim of this machine is to prove experimentally that the motion of extremely hot gases can be contained and controlled. A gas which is heated above a few thousand degrees Celsius (centigrade), reorganizes itself into a new state of matter called plasma. Thereby scientific man recreates an action that already exists in the universe and has been observed by astronomers, including for example in our Sun. The research facility at Greifswald will be able to keep within its experimental container a plasma of 100 million degrees Celsius, making those physical processes of nature controllable by the human mind, which are otherwise the "daily business" of the stars.

These experiments are being conducted to prove that the construction of plasma power plants, in which extremely high amounts of energy can be harvested out of the minute components of a hydrogen atom, is possible. Where there is water there is always hydrogen, a fraction of which shows a different atomic structure. These hydrogen isotopes have the characteristic that, when exposed to such a hot plasma environment, they will "melt together" the fusion process.

The fusion process gives birth to a new physical element, which in this case is helium. The crux of the matter is this: When this action takes place, a neutron is shot out of the nucleus of the hydrogen isotopes, carrying with it an astonishing amount of energy. The energy of these neutrons can be converted into heat, which can be used to put turbines and generators into motion to produce electricity. Just 80 grams of hydrogen isotopes can generate the same amount of energy as one billion grams (or 1,000 metric tons), of coal. This energy, obtainable from an element that surrounds us everywhere, has an energy-flux density 12 million times higher—when carried by the neutrons shooting out of the fused nuclei—than coal, which we have to dig out of the earth with immense physical effort, and load into hundreds of freight cars.

Of course, society has to invest significant resources into the realization and general use of newly discovered technologies; however, once these technologies become a common tool in our spectrum of applications, mankind enters a new world. The proper term for a mode of operation by society which consciously drives this process forward, is scientific culture, or progress.

How the Plasma Is Contained

Plasmas move in a circle in most containment devices. Nature has however somehow decreed that a plasma, bounded by its characteristics, will not choose a perfect circle, but rather a more complex, ring-shaped form. Because of its electromagnetic charge, the containment of the plasma in the vessel can be achieved by

Max Planck Institute for Plasma Physics/Wolfgang Filser
Part of the plasma vessel during fabrication. Construction of the device in time-lapse video is shown here.

strong magnets, which will also prevent the plasma from touching the walls of the container. The Greifswald fusion project has been named Wendelstein 7-X, and its machine is called a stellarator. In a recent public presentation, its scientific director, Professor Thomas Klinger, described it as an "optimized torus with curves and bumps." He then compared the shape of the stellarator's magnetic field with that of a solar protuberance, whose ejections resemble complex curved structures, as if nature were "looking to follow a suitable magnetic field form." The shape and arrangement of the Wendelstein 7-X magnets determine the shape of the magnetic field. This guarantees that the plasma will take the optimal shape for achieving the required long-lasting stability.

Liquid helium in an oversized refrigerator called a cryostat is used to cool the magnets, so that they are super-conductive even under high voltage. A generator of 10-million watt microwaves is used to heat the hydrogen gas until it ionizes, becoming hydrogen plasma. The stellarator has a diameter of 16 meters, weighs 725 tons, and has 50 specially arranged, ring-shaped magnets, as well as 20 more flat magnets. The plasma vessel has a volume of 30 cubic meters.

This highly complex machine is being operated by specially trained personnel in a control center, whose system consists of a great number of monitors showing the temperature—approximately minus 270 degrees Celsius—and the electrical current—about 13,000 Amperes—in the magnetic coils. Other monitors show the state of the vacuum pump and the security system.

In July 2015, a series of tests of the magnets was successfully completed. Further experiments confirmed that the computer-simulated magnetic field lines and the actual field lines in the machine were congruent. After some readjustments by the engineers, the first test plasma was produced on December 10, 2015, when about one milligram of helium was fed into the evacuated plasma vessel. On Feb. 3, the first hydrogen plasma was produced, which marked the start of the series of scientific investigations which will run until 2020. The aim of the final tests will be to produce a stable hydrogen plasma for 30 minutes without interruption. A visibly excited German Chancellor Angela Merkel (PhD in quantum chemistry) pushed the button to initiate a 60-second countdown sequence, after she spoke about the need for fundamental research and scientific breakthroughs as a basis for a progressing living standard. The audience on Feb. 3 was made up of many leading scientific, industrial, and academic institutions, including a representative of the U.S. Department of Energy, which had contributed $20 million to this enterprise.

Project Stellarator

Initially there was a lot of controversy surrounding the stellarator concept, says project director Professor Klinger, because the first models and tests with the optimal shape of the magnetic field were a failure. Almost all the laboratories in the world "threw their stellarators in the garbage," he continues. Only the "stubborn Germans" and the Japanese continued their research. The mathematics and physics of the complex systems were extraordinarily difficult, until faster computers made the simulation of their magnetic field lines possible.

Today it is generally acknowledged that it was right to pursue parallel scientific avenues, and not to abandon the development of the stellarator, despite all the setbacks, because it offers advantages when compared with the other major fusion device, the doughnut-shaped Tokamak model,— such as the continuous operation of the plasma. Says Klinger: "We had split from the commonly available concepts for the magnetic coils. Then we looked into the computer and asked what the shape of the magnetic field should be, for one that the plasma actually would like to have. We got the result, and calculated backwards to determine the shape of the magnets. We don't have to call into question the shape of the magnetic coils any longer, because they are now determined by the physics of the plasma."

The construction of the buildings in Greifswald began in 1996, and the first magnet was delivered in 2004. Between 2005 and 2013, all of the approximately one million parts of the system were assembled, the coils were tested, and the final welding was done. With costs a little higher than one billion Euros, the stellarator is an official major project of the German industrial and scientific community. Most of the 200 engineers, 200 physicists, and 60 additional staff are driven by idealism and excitement about this project, says Professor Klinger. Eighty percent of the financial support came from federal and local state funds, and only 20% from the European Commission.

Some international experts claim that this machine could only have been built by Germans with their "clockmaker mentality," as their distinctive sense of precision is whimsically labeled. Nevertheless, the Wendelstein 7-X is not a particular German path, but an international lead project, where scientists from all over the world will be working.

A New Paradigm

The stellarator is a groundbreaking concept, which poses a fundamental question to us: Will human civilization seize this opportunity to turn wholeheartedly towards rational progress, or will we end up in certain tragedy by dismissing or even refusing it altogether? The reorganization of of our productive economy to the level of a plasma-fusion based economy, demands of us a dramatic shift to an entirely new direction in our cultural outlook. We have to let go of a society driven by irrational entertainment and anti-technological hysteria.

Plasma research will open up the possibility of an unprecedented thrust of innovation in machine-tool design, micro-electronics, medicine, and many more fields of activity which still have to be defined. The "green technologies" with their extremely low energy-flux density have maneuvered our society into an obvious dead-end. We have to force nothing less than a complete change in paradigm, while all of our popular convictions, which have gotten us into this mess today, have to be brought into question. A broad and open discussion about this must be initiated now, because this is about the future of our human species.

REAL SCIENCE

Einstein's Method of the 'Thought Experiment'

by Judy Hodgkiss

Jan. 31—Even the best of our modern scientists speak of Einstein's scientific discoveries as if those ideas could be encapsulated in the mathematics associated with those discoveries. For example:

• Atomic physicists repeat the mantra of "$E=mc^2$," as if that "formula" had emerged from Einstein's head as an isolated idea;

• Quantum physicists speak of Einstein's radiation equations, while totally ignoring Einstein's Riemannian hypothesis of the electron's quantum action;

• Astronomers today insist that it was the "mathematics" of general relativity that predicted A. Eddington's demonstration of the ability of the sun's gravity to bend starlight;

• Those same scientists insist that it was general relativity's "mathematics" that predicted such astrophysical phenomena as black holes.

The source of our problem here is the ubiquitous influence of Bertrand Russell's reductionist educational methods in the physics departments of the Twentieth Century.[1] We find that, today,

Commenting later on his effort at four-five years of age to figure out how a compass worked, Einstein concluded "Something deeply hidden had to be behind things." From 12-16 years of age he studied advanced mathematics using books "that were not too particular regarding logical rigor, but that permitted the principal ideas to stand out clearly," he said. He is 14 years old in this picture.

even those researchers who might genuinely admire Albert Einstein have no comprehension of the nature of the methods he used to make his discoveries.

Compounding the problem is that Einstein, himself, never comprehensively described his own methodology. We find only an occasional glimpse, here and there, in his many books, lectures, and articles, as to how his mind actually worked. He is especially difficult to fathom when it comes to how he discovered the 1915 general relativity out of the preliminary form of special relativity, which he had discovered in 1905.

Here we will focus on the method of thinking that Einstein had called a *Gedankenexperiment*, a "thought experiment." We concede, of course, that the "thought experiment" was not an invention of Einstein's: It has always been the true scientific method of the great thinkers from Plato of the ancient Greeks to Bernard Riemann of Nineteenth-century Germany. But the spectacular aspect of Einstein's experimental "thoughts" was, that they were specific types of images which, understood in the proper context, were capable of overthrowing centuries of Newtonian reductionist

1. http://www.larouchepub.com/other/2016/4305russell_made_us_stupid.html

dogma, and, at the same time, millennia of Euclidean dogma.

Riding a Light Wave

Einstein famously said that "imagination is more important than knowledge." Certainly, the attainment of knowledge will always be a prerequisite for resolving certain questions in a finalized form; but, imagining the right question in the first place is a much more important—and rare—capability.

Einstein called the initial process a certain kind of "wondering." In his *Autobiographical Notes*,[2] Einstein recalled:

> I have no doubt that our thinking goes on for the most part without use of signs (words) and beyond that to a considerable degree unconsciously. For how, otherwise, should it happen that sometimes we "wonder" quite spontaneously about some experience? This "wondering" appears to occur when an experience comes into conflict with a world of concepts already sufficiently fixed within us. Whenever such a conflict is experienced sharply and intensively it reacts back upon our world of thought in a decisive way. The development of the world of thought is in a certain sense a continuous flight from "wonder."
>
> A wonder of this kind I experienced as a child of four or five years when my father showed me a compass. That this needle behaved in such a determined way did not at all fit into the kind of occurrences that could find a place in the unconscious world of concepts (efficacy produced by direct 'touch'). I can still remember—or at least believe I can remember—that this experience made a deep and lasting impression upon me. Something deeply hidden had to be behind things.

And, in 1895, long before Einstein had attained a level of education thorough enough to explore the question in depth, he had had an intimation—at the age of *sixteen*—of what became his theory of special relativ-

Einstein came to the conclusion that the "dogmatic rigidity" with which physics held on to Newton's laws as if they had been "created by God," and that solutions could be made by means of deduction, had to be overthrown as the foundation for all physics, which led to his development of relativity theory. In response to Einstein's work, in 1919 The Times *in Britain warned in a headline: "Newtonian ideas Overthrown." At right, Euclid, Newton's predecessor as a deductive "thinker."*

ity, as laid out in 1905. Einstein described that 10-year-long struggle:

> At the age of twelve through sixteen I familiarized myself with the elements of mathematics, including the principles of differential and integral calculus. In doing so I had the good fortune of encountering books that were not too particular regarding logical rigor, but that permitted the principal ideas to stand out clearly ....
>
> At the age of seventeen, I entered the Polytechnic Institute of Zurich as a student of mathematics and physics. There I had excellent teachers ... so that I should have been able to obtain a mathematical training in depth. I worked most of the time in the physical laboratory, however, fascinated by the direct contact with experience ....
>
> "[Perhaps] my intuition was not strong enough in the field of mathematics to differentiate clearly the fundamentally important, that which is really basic, from the rest of the more or less dispensable erudition... [In physics,] however, I soon learned to scent out that which might lead to fundamentals and to turn aside from everything else, from the multitude of things that clutter up the mind and divert it from the essentials ....
>
> Now, to the field of physics as it presented itself at that time. In spite of great productivity in particulars, dogmatic rigidity prevailed in mat-

---

2. Einstein, *Autobiographical Notes,* translated and edited by Paul Arthur Schilpp, 1949.

ters of principle: In the beginning (if there was such a thing), God created Newton's laws of motion together with the necessary masses and forces. This is all; everything beyond this follows from the development of appropriate mathematical methods by means of deduction . . . .

We must not be surprised, therefore, that, so to speak, all physicists of the previous century saw in classical mechanics a firm and definitive foundation for all physics, indeed for the whole of natural science, and that they never grew tired in their attempts to base Maxwell's theory of electromagnetism, which, in the meantime, was slowly beginning to win out, upon mechanics as well. Even Maxwell and H. Hertz, who in retrospect are properly recognized as those who shook the faith in mechanics as the final basis of all physical thinking, in their conscious thinking consistently held fast to mechanics as the confirmed basis of physics . . . .

The most fascinating subject at the time that I was a student was Maxwell's theory. What made this theory appear revolutionary was the transition from [Newton's] action at a distance to fields as the fundamental variables . . . .

[But it became] clear to me as long ago as shortly after 1900, i.e., shortly after Planck's trailblazing work, that neither mechanics nor electrodynamics could (except in limiting cases) claim exact validity. Gradually I despaired of the possibility of discovering the true laws by means of constructive efforts based on known facts. The longer and the more desperately I tried, the more I came to the conviction that only the discovery of a universal formal principle could lead us to assured results…How then could such a universal principle be found? After ten years of reflection such a principle resulted from a paradox upon which I had already hit at the age of sixteen: If I pursue a beam of light with the velocity "c," I should observe such a beam of light as an electromagnetic field at rest though spatially oscillating. There seems to be no such thing, however, neither on the basis of experience nor according to Maxwell's equations. From the very beginning it appeared to me intuitively clear that, judged from the standpoint of such an observer, everything would have to happen according to the same laws as for an observer who, relative to the earth, was

Einstein said that after Max Planck's "trailblazing work," he gradually came to the conclusion that he could not come to a solution only "based on known facts."

at rest. For how should the first observer know, or be able to determine, that he is in a state of fast uniform motion?

One sees that in this paradox the germ of the special relativity theory is already contained. Today everyone knows, of course, that all attempts to clarify this paradox satisfactorily were condemned to failure as long as the axiom of the absolute character of time, or of simultaneity, was rooted unrecognized in the unconscious. To recognize clearly this axiom and its arbitrary character already implies the essentials of the solution of the problem.

And, so it was that from there, after reflecting on the *Gedankenexperiment* of his youth—of the *16-year-old Einstein*—that the *26-year-old* Einstein could then proceed to proclaim his new theory of relativity: Einstein found that not only were space and time variable in any calculations concerning action in the physical universe, but also that *time* varied according to the reference frame, i.e., that there was no absolute "time," no absolute notion of simultaneity; but that "time" itself was relative to the reference frame of the observer.

The only thing "constant" in this system is the speed of light.[3] As for the idea of "catching up" with a light wave, where the observer might see an electromagnetic field in a state of rest: the very idea would violate the "law" of conservation of energy. Therefore, that principle of "conservation of energy" must be fused with the principle of the "conservation of linear momentum," whereby the inert "mass" of an isolated body is identical with its "energy." Here, mass is eliminated as an *independent* concept: hence, we come to $E=mc^2$ (or, $m=E/c^2$).

All of this was verified when, with the development of the particle accelerator, a particle accelerating to near the speed of light was found to be gaining "mass" as it accelerated, as measured by the observer, who was at rest. And, inversely, as when a radioactive substance loses a minute amount of mass that is proportional to the *energy* required for it to eject its decay substance. And, of course, mass can be converted to energy in an explosive manner, with nuclear reactions.

A Man Falling From a Roof

By 1907, after the dust had settled around the 1905 publication of what was later called, the "special" theory of relativity, Einstein began the difficult process of "generalizing" those special cases to which his theory had been limited, i.e., going from a system where observers were always in *uniform* motion in relation to each other, but to now expand it to include *all* cases of relative motion between the observers, however arbitrary the motion might be.

At the same time that Einstein was working on this problem, he was contemplating a related one: why did Newton's force laws seem to work, even though they violated the theory of relativity? Newton believed in the action-at-a-distance law of gravity, whereby bodies could sense changes in motions of another body exerting a gravitational pull on it, as if the timing of its "reacting" was *simultaneous* with the generating action itself. *Gravity,* itself, had to be redefined—Einstein would later call it an "apparent" force, not a "real" one in the sense of Newton's laws of mechanics.

As we will see later, Einstein ultimately found that, in

order to resolve these paradoxes, he must replace Euclidean with Riemannian geometry, to which he was introduced in 1912.[4] But it was even before that, back in 1907, that Einstein had the original *Gedankenexperiment*, that spurred him in the direction of the Riemannian solution. Einstein describes that *Gedankenexperiment,* that moment of insight, as the "happiest thought" of his life. Below are several different descriptions by Einstein of how that "happiest" of thought experiments came to him:

"I was sitting in a chair in the patent office at Zurich [where he was still working at the time] when all of a sudden a thought occurred to me: If a person falls freely he will not feel his own weight. I was startled. This simple thought made a deep impression on me. It impelled me toward a theory of gravitation."[5]

"I was occupied (in 1907) with a comprehensive survey of the special theory for the 'Yearbook for Radioactivity and Electronics.' I also had to attempt to modify Newton's theory of gravitation in such a way that its laws fitted into the theory. Attempts along these lines showed the practicality of this enterprise, but did not satisfy me, because they had to be based on physical hypotheses that were not well-founded. Then there came to me the happiest thought of my life in the following form:

> Like the electric field generated by electromagnetic induction...the gravitational field only has a relative existence. Because, for an observer freely falling from the roof of a house, during his fall there exists—at least in the immediate vicinity— no gravitational field. Indeed, if the observer lets go of any objects, relative to him they remain in a state of rest or uniform motion, independently of their particular chemical or physical composition

3. That is, the speed of light in a perfect vacuum.

4. From Cornelius Lanczos, *Albert Einstein and the Cosmic World Order,* New York, John Wiley and Sons, 1965:
"Riemann saw further than his contemporaries ... [Riemann] points out that some day the physicist of the future may see himself compelled to go beyond the framework of Newtonian concepts. His work has purely the purpose of clearing the way to a broader approach so that, when that time comes, science should not be hamstrung by traditional prejudices. No words could have expressed more adequately the historical destiny which was in store for Einstein.
"Riemann's prophetic utterance was spoken at the end of his 'inaugural address,' given on the occasion of his election to the mathematical faculty of the University of Göttingen (1854)... [His advisor], Gauss, found the topic, entitled, 'On the hypotheses which are at the foundation of geometry,' particularly to his taste ...."
5. Dec. 14, 1922 lecture, "How I Created the Theory of Relativity," Kyoto University, Japan.

[note by AE: air resistance is naturally ignored in this argument]. The observer is thus justified in interpreting his state as being at rest."[6]

"Imagine a great lift at the top of a skyscraper much higher than any real one. Suddenly the cable supporting the lift breaks and the lift falls freely toward the ground. Observers in the lift are performing experiments during the fall. In describing them, we need not bother about air resistance or friction, for we may disregard their existence under our idealized conditions. One of the observers takes a handkerchief and a watch from his pocket and drops them. What happens to these two bodies? For the outside observer, who is looking through the window of the lift, both handkerchief and watch fall toward the ground in exactly the same way, with the same acceleration. We remember that the acceleration of a falling body is quite independent of its mass and that it was this fact which revealed the equality of gravitational and inertial mass. We also remember that the equality of the two masses, gravitational and inertial, was quite accidental from the point of view of classical [Newtonian] mechanics and played no role in its structure. Here, however, this equality reflected in the equal acceleration of all falling bodies is essential and forms the basis of our whole argument."[7]

Thus, Einstein—long before there was space travel and the demonstration of "weightlessness" in space—conceived of the freely falling body as having no sensation of a gravitational pull. The next step was to imagine the lift in space, outside of the earth's gravity, and being accelerated upwards with the uniform acceleration of 32 feet per second squared, thereby simulating earth's gravitational pull. The observer inside the elevator could not tell if he were stationary on earth and feeling the pull of its gravity, or whether it was merely his relative motion that caused him to feel the sensation of gravitation pull.

Einstein concluded from all this, with the help of Riemannian geometry, that planets do not carve out their elliptical paths around the sun because they feel a "force" acting upon them; but that the planets are merely following the straight path defined by their inertial momentum, and that the straight line that they seem to be following carries them around a curved portion of space defined by the mass of the sun.

---

6. 1920 unpublished draft of article for *Nature* magazine.
7. Einstein and Infeld, *The Evolution of Physics*, 1938. A note of caution: The wording here is more likely to be that of Infeld, than Einstein.

Don't 'Just Do the Math'

One additional aspect of the "lift" thought experiment should be mentioned, in order to dispel the notion that it was general relativity's "mathematics" that predicted the results of the 1919 Eddington experiment that showed starlight is bent by the gravitational pull of the sun. Again, it was a thought experiment—this time an extension of the accelerating lift experiment—which predicted that such a phenomenon would exist. Here Einstein imagines a light beam which cuts across the lift from one side to the other as the lift is accelerating. An outside observer would see that that beam had come across initially intersecting the lift at its center-point on the left side. But as the lift moves upward, the beam continues on towards the right side of the lift, but changing constantly in relation to the floor of the lift. The beam will carve out a (curved) path, relative to its initial crossing point of the moving lift, and will finish crossing the path of the lift, on its right side, at a point much closer to its floor.

Because this happens in the reference frame of the simulation of gravity (in the accelerating lift), it must also be the case that the same thing will happen in the stationary reference frame on earth in response to "real" gravity: light must be bent as it traverses a gravitational field. But—one might object—isn't there a problem with the idea of gravity being able to have an effect on an electromagnetic wave? Einstein answers:

But there is, fortunately, a grave fault in the reasoning of [such a person], which saves our previous conclusion. He said: 'A beam of light is weightless and, therefore, will not be affected by the gravitational field.' This cannot be right! A beam of light carries energy and energy has mass. But every inertial mass is attracted by the gravitational field, as inertial and gravitational masses are equivalent. A beam of light will bend in a gravitational field exactly as a body would if thrown horizontally with a velocity equal to that of light. If [such an] observer had reasoned correctly and had taken into account the bending of light rays in a gravitational field, then his results would have been exactly the same as those of an outside observer.

The gravitational field of the earth is, of course, too weak for the bending of light rays in it to be proved directly, by experiment. But the famous experiments [the Eddington experi-

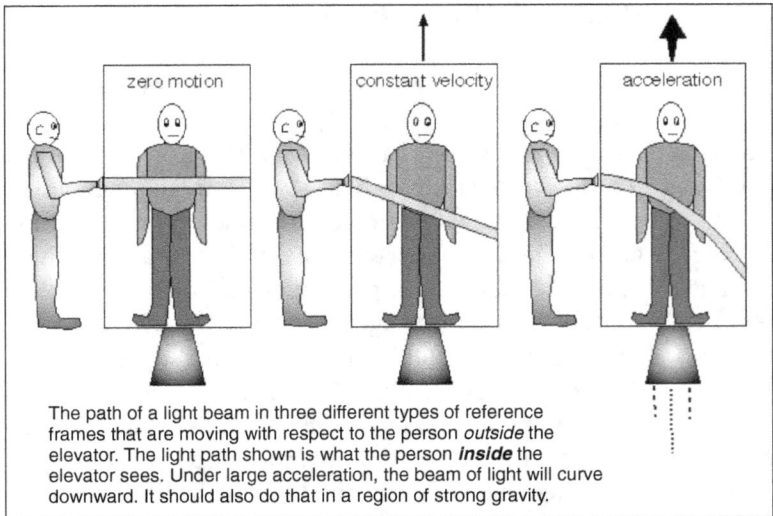

The path of a light beam in three different types of reference frames that are moving with respect to the person *outside* the elevator. The light path shown is what the person **inside** the elevator sees. Under large acceleration, the beam of light will curve downward. It should also do that in a region of strong gravity.

The lift (elevator) thought experiment demonstrates Einstein's thought process.

ments] performed during the solar eclipses show, conclusively though indirectly, the influence of a gravitational field on the path of a light ray.[8]

Another myth that should be dispelled here is that the "mathematics" of general relativity has "predicted" such phenomena as "black holes." Einstein made clear, on more than one occasion, that the formal mathematics of general relativity is incomplete, and therefore liable to breaking down.[9] Einstein explains that, although he was able to find a Riemannian geometry for matter/space/time applicable to gravitational fields, he could *not* discover how to apply it to electromagnetic fields. Hence,

_____

8. *Ibid.*

9. From *Autobiographical Notes:*

"Not for a moment…did I doubt that this formulation was merely a makeshift in order to give the general principle of relativity a preliminary closed-form expression. For it was essentially no more than a theory of the gravitational field, which was isolated somewhat artificially from a total field of as yet unknown structure …

"The *universal* law of physical space must be a generalization of the [previous field-free case]. I assumed that there are two steps of generalization: [emphasis in the original]

a) the pure gravitational field

b) the general field (which is also to include quantities that somehow correspond to the electromagnetic field).

"The case (a) was characterized by the fact that the field can still be represented by a Riemann metric …. [But] it seemed hopeless to me at the time to venture the attempt of representing the total field (b) and to ascertain field laws for it. I preferred, therefore, to set up a preliminary formal frame for the representation of the entire physical reality; this was necessary in order to be able to investigate, at least preliminarily, the effectiveness of the basic idea of general relativity."

Einstein's lifetime search for a unified field theory.

Einstein's mathematics will predictably break down (the equations going to infinity) anywhere that strong electromagnetic fields are encountered—as is the case with the entire spectrum of phenomena which ranges from black holes, to active galactic nuclei, to quasars. None of these phenomena are merely gravitationally anomalous—which might indeed test the true limits of general relativity theory as it relates to gravity—but these phenomena are all energetically anomalous, and therefore Einstein's *incomplete* theory of relativity cannot tell you anything definitive about them.

Unfortunately, there are modern astronomers who jump to the conclusion that these energetic phenomena prove relativity theory, in its premises, to be wrong; but these gentlemen are only proving their ignorance of the true nature of relativity theory and of the Leibniz/Gauss/Riemann tradition upon which it is based.

For us to move beyond Einstein, to a comprehensive Larouchian/Vernadskian/Riemannian notion of an anti-entropic universe, we must thoroughly familiarize ourselves with the method of the "thought experiment." And we must never become embroiled in arguments that revolve around interpretations of the "mathematics of Einstein."

Instead, we might consider a "thought experiment" connected with an hypothesis of how electromagnetism (light) mysteriously interacts with chlorophyll. Consider that kind of interaction, and then compare the way that gravity interacts with biological systems, where we find nothing nearly so stark or so interesting. That gives us a clue as to why gravitational fields are more easily modeled compared to electromagnetic fields. One approach that might help us in this effort, is to look at Einstein's attempt to develop a Riemannian model for the electron's quantum behavior, which was presented in a largely neglected lecture in 1917.[10]

We must learn to think as Einstein thought. Then, bringing in our LaRouchian perspective, we may find our own happy *Gedankenexperiment*.

_____

10 . "On the Quantum Theorem of Sommerfeld and Epstein," May 11, 1917, in *The Collected Papers of Albert Einstein*, vol. 6, Princeton University Press, 1997.

Every Day Counts
In Today's Showdown
To Save Civilization

That's why you need EIR's **Daily Alert Service**, a strategic overview compiled with the input of Lyndon LaRouche, and delivered to your email 5 days a week.

For example: On Jan. 7, EIR's Daily Alert featured the British hand behind the pattern of global provocations toward war. Of special note is British Intelligence's role in instigating the Saudi Kingdom's attempt to set off a Sunni-Shia war. This religious war has been the intent of British strategy since the Blair-Bush attack on Iraq in 2003.

We also uniquely update you regularly on the progress toward the release of the suppressed 28 pages of the Congressional Inquiry on 9/11, which would expose the Saudi role.

Every edition highlights the reality of the impending financial crash/bail-in policies that would realize the British goal of mass depopulation.

This is intelligence you need to act on, if we are going to survive as a nation and a species. Can you really afford to be without it?

THURSDAY, JANUARY 7, 2016

Volume 2, Number 97

EIR Daily Alert Service

P.O. Box 17390, WASHINGTON, DC 20041-0390

- British Crown Pushing War and Genocide in 2016
- Financial Mudslide Goes On; Monetarist Tyranny Gloats over Bail-Ins
- Moody's Downgrades Portugal's Novo Banco
- Puerto Rico's Default: It's Every Vulture for Himself
- Wide Glass-Steagall Debate Set Off Again by Sanders Speech
- MI6 Mouthpiece Evans-Pritchard Touts Persian Gulf Chaos
- North Korea Tests a Miniaturized Hydrogen Bomb
- Uighur Terrorists Found in Indonesia
- Foreign Investors Are Flocking In to China

EDITORIAL

British Crown Pushing War and Genocide in 2016

Get Rid of Obama and the British Monarchy to Have A New Chance for Mankind

Jan. 28—Edited excerpts from the Fireside Chat with Lyndon LaRouche of Jan. 28.

Host John Ascher: Good evening everyone, this is John Ascher. Hi, Lyn! We're here for our special emergency discussion, as you called for earlier this week....

Lyndon LaRouche: I hear you.

Ascher: Given the recent developments, Lyn, before we begin questions, do you have any remarks to make?

LaRouche: The question is this: There's things we don't know, but they are going to happen anyway. But we just have a lack of certainty among some issues, because we're not in an effective place to take on everything all at the same time. But there's no question that those of us who are intent on surviving this situation, surviving this period of history, are going to work with us, because it's the only way we have available to do any good.

I'm not being pessimistic at all, because it's possible that we could bring something off, which would actually shut down some of the things that are actually being put into place; it's possible. What we have to do is concentrate on those conceptions, those options which do exist, and concentrate our attention on those options which we know are of a type which *would* be perfected, rather than trying to swarm around and trying to feel our way through the darkness. I don't believe in feeling through the darkness. I believe in finding loopholes in which we can make a progress.

It's like the military thing, you know; troops were out there in the field sometimes, waiting for the signal to enter combat, and it probably didn't happen at that time. But the point is, whenever this thing is in place, whenever it's in place as it is now, then you have to react accordingly. And I'm ready to react accordingly.

There are things that can be done, which should be effective in dumping Obama from the Presidency of the United States. That is the only thing which will save the United States from self-destruction. So that's what I'm working on, and that's what I'm concentrating: It's the only thing that *could* work, and should work.

They Support the Disease

Question: Lyn, we have a question which is related to the physical breakdown of the economy, which comes from a longtime activist and supporter in Connecticut. And he gives a lengthy question about having

The Black Death was the new disease of Fourteenth-century Europe.

been in India in 1965, and he was in the medical field at the time, and talks about the role of DDT.

His concern is this, Lyn. You probably have heard there is now a new deadly virus, that there's been a health emergency declared concerning, called the Zika virus; which is spreading in South and Central America, and it's affecting newborn infants. And it's been clear that the only way to destroy this is to get rid of the mosquitoes, and Jim asks, "why can't we use DDT, and why haven't we been using DDT?"

LaRouche: The answer is very simple: They don't want to cure the disease. They don't want to cure it! You have to realize that the British Empire, in particular, that is all of the leaders of the British Empire, and all of the people associated with that; and many in various parts of South America are for the same thing, *for* the spread of this kind of disease. Not by saying they want that disease to come, but because they're against allowing the *cure* of that disease to be supplied.

The point is, we have to realize that you cannot do a one-shot fix-it, not in terms of what's going on now. You have the British Empire, which is the dominant feature in the trans-Atlantic community. You have to remove that element, that part, the British Empire part, you have to *shut it down*.

Now, if you look at these stories, what you see in the United States itself is that you've got all these people who are part of the support for the wrong people. People who are part of the whole speculation system.

Therefore, *these* are the issues. You have to remove the issues which *cause* this threat. And there is very little attention being given to the possibility of saving people from these kinds of frightening,— terrifying, often,— diseases. These are new diseases, in general history, and there's nothing being done which portends to be able to fight these diseases, because the relevant people don't want to fight these diseases! They like the diseases!

It doesn't mean they like it personally, but it means their determination is to *reduce the human population throughout the planet*! To cut down the number of living people, in order to make a cheaper world. A world that doesn't work for mankind.

I mean, this has been done before; there has been mass death induced in periods of history, because a body, which sometimes will often call itself devoted to being religious, will generally almost wipe out the entire population of nations. And that's history.

CC/ohad

"The Governor of California, the current one, destroys the people of California." Here, Governor Jerry Brown.

So the thing you have to do is realize what has been done, in the way that in many nations in South America have toppled themselves into that kind of category, who are going to spread disease, deadly disease throughout South America and elsewhere. So therefore, the problem is, we discuss the wrong thing. We protect the disease, and abhor the cure.

Twentieth Century Traditions

Question: This is J— from Anaheim. I had a question for Mr. LaRouche. I'm concerned with the mainstream media narrative, and its power of suggestion, and how the American public is rather uninformed on many things. I wanted to see, from you, in your opinion would it be worthwhile to pursue an effort by getting organized and having some youth organization involved, to nationalize the media? Or would it be a worthless effort?

LaRouche: I don't know about that particular formulation as a proposition. I simply think that the way we have to organize the population, is in several ways. Now, the problem is, in part, the fact of the quality of education and education-like experiences in the United States, since the beginning of Bertrand Russell's arrival on the scene in the Twentieth Century. And there has been constantly a destruction, a destructive force of corruption throughout the planet—more or less throughout most of the planet, especially the trans-Atlantic region. Now, that's happened

And if we continue on that course, which has become tradition, the Twentieth-century principle,— if you follow the Twentieth-century principle,— the way that schoolchildren, or even pre-school children believe today, in general, there will probably be very few schoolchildren who have any minds left at all. Their minds have been already destroyed by the inception of an element of what must be called "disease." And even little children are destroying themselves, as a package, because they don't know what it is they have to do. Therefore, they lead themselves to destruction.

And our problem is that today, given the degeneration of the opinion of the American people since the beginning of the Twentieth Century, the degeneration which came on after Franklin Roosevelt was removed from power, that disease and the things which are like it which have come into play,— like against some great leaders who were exceptions,— and you are at a point now, that if you want to behave the way that your teacher tells you, in general, the way you're educated, the way you're informed, your taste in music, so-called music, all of these things *lead toward your own self-destruction.*

Now, that's not a final word. The point is, if we are actually intelligent, we are going to reject what we are told in today's schools, say in the public schools in California; they are poison. They tend to destroy the people of California. The governor of California, the current one, destroys the people of California. That's what happens.

So the point is, we have to make a distinction between issues and principles. Principle is health; the alternative is speculation. We have to change our behavior. And it's not too hard to do so when push comes to shove. But the problem is that you try to submit to what you call a "popular opinion" and say, "I don't want to be opposed to popular opinion, I must respect popular opinion." And Satan is just outside the door there, waiting to pull you in. And that's the best way to understand that.

We've Got to Grow Up

Question: Hello Lyndon, this is J— from Massachusetts. Just speaking of India made me think, how did the British control such a vast population as the country of India? But I wanted to ask you, also, is there any chance to be a super-delegate that would support O'Malley? Any group at all, in the Democratic Party or in Congress?

LaRouche: I would not worry too much about him, O'Malley. The man is good. Now, let me just get to the truth of these matters. I had a discussion going on around this issue just recently, and what I did is, I led the enemy, which is Hillary and Sanders, and I led them down the line by provoking them, and they decided they were going to go all the way and were going to make sure that the persons that I supported should *never* be elected. Well, they did that!

Now, what they've done, is what? In the period where they think they've conquered everything, they've effected just the opposite effect. By being suckers to support Hillary and Sanders, both, they made both of them absolute fools. And that's the point.

If you want to get into the business of politics and you want to win, that is win, not in the sense of stealing something, but win in the sense of winning something that's worth winning,— and what these guys did, when they bought into my trap, the trap I set for them, and went for 100% wiping out of O'Malley, you didn't destroy O'Malley! You destroyed yourselves.

Question: I have a question that just came in which is kind of in the similar vein, but dealing with the—I hate to say it—but the Republican side of the Presidential election. And this gentleman, it's a very, very long statement, but I'll try to get some sense of it: He refers to first the fact that Rand Paul has left the Presidential race and said this is sad because he was the only hope that we had. And then he talks about the fact that Ted Cruz and Donald Trump are only there to eliminate Dr. Ben Carson and Rand Paul from getting the Republican nomination.

Let me put it to you this way, because it's extremely lengthy: He's very concerned that Jeb Bush is still going to somehow come in from the outside. I'll put it to you this way—let me try to put a little more positively what this gentleman hopefully is referring to: Is there any hope at all that something could come out of the Republican Party under these circumstances?

LaRouche: Well, that's a strong question. It's not impossible, if you get a turnaround. Look, what you've got is the Senate and the House of Representatives are pretty much, I would say, fair imitations of whorehouses. They may not intend to do that, but that's the effect of what they do. I mean—Trump? My God, this man Trump! Do you think he's even human? If you

"What Putin has done ... is a miracle."

know his record, this man's an absolute fool, and a fatuous fool, and he has very bad antecedents, has very bad habits, and he shouldn't be in any place outside of a circus! And I don't know if the circus would take him on.

So what we have to do, is we have to realize that we are human beings. We are supposed to have intellectual capabilities to see through some problems, some situations. We're supposed to, thereby find a way to make a contribution to society which will be beneficial to mankind in future, in some way, and so forth. Well: that's it, isn't it? That's the issue!

Now, it's true. What do we do? We buy these guys! We buy the Republicans! We buy the Democrats! We buy them like animals, selling them as if they were some kind of a toad or something, that had to hop along there; and we had one toad was a Republican and the other toad was a Democrat.

No, this whole thing is mythological. If the people of the United States,— and I think they can, but they're going to have to do a little painful experience on this one,— if we want to do it,— and we have friends, in China, big friends; *big* friends! The biggest friends you could ever imagine, China! Russia: Russia is the most effective political institution, in terms of the planet right now. What Putin has done in his leadership in the reconstruction of Russia, is a miracle! A scientific miracle, of science, of physical science. And this is reality!

So the idea that you have to know who's which guy's rear end you're going to kiss, that is not really a very good standard for choice of candidate.

No, we've got to grow up. And what I represent,— and some of you know what I represent. I think that what I represent, is pretty close to the right thing. And I think if we're smart, we're going to try the taste of my pudding, at least a little bit.

The Basis of Mankind

Question: This is R— from South Dakota. I just picked up a copy of John Perkins' book today, the *New Confessions of an Economic Hit Man*, and in there he refers to going back to the '50s and '60s, when the American public had a sense of morality. And in there, he's talking about the modern, the new economic hit man, and he lists Tom Daschle, the former Senator from South Dakota here, and Chris Dodd. And he goes on to list a bunch of the Republicans that he now considers to be economic hit men, and which includes Newt Gingrich, Phil Gramm, Chuck Hagel, Trent Lott, Warren Rudman, and the list goes on past that.

But anyway, that gives you a sense of how these guys have degenerated. Tom Daschle, in the '80s and the '90s, used to listen to LaRouche's ideas. He put together a proposal with Congressman Bingham, back in the '80s, that was patterned after the LaRouche program. And what he turned into today, is totally despicable and disgraceful.

And I think back to the '50s and '60s when I was a boy and a young man, and how my family, around the dinner table after church on Sunday, would have a political discussion, and by the time they got done talking and thrashing over these guys, a guy like Daschle, I mean, we would have been looking for pitchforks and a rope to hang the bastard, when he set foot in South Dakota.

What can we do, to re-instill in the American people, a sense of morality again? What specifically can I do, or anybody listening, what do you think they can do, Lyn, to re-instill that?

LaRouche: It's very simple: I'm doing it. The recipe,— I'm doing it. I know the facts, probably better than anyone, of what these facts are, and it's not just because of my old age, but it's because of my experience. Remember, I've been through the whole thing. I've been a significant figure in many countries over this period. I have a pretty accurate record, in terms of these kinds of facts. And I don't think you can simply pick something out of the basket, and say, "this is the new prophet we're going to adopt, or the thing we're going to do next."

No. We're working at it. Look, we are organizing in Manhattan, for example, and we have regular events which occur in Manhattan as such, and in the environs of Manhattan as such, in terms of the revival of Classical musical compositions' performance; of discoveries, *re*-discoveries of scientific principles. And the great mass of people, according to the popular total of things, are stupid, idiotic.

Now, what's wrong? Why would people who wish to be effective as human beings, why would they want to build up something that's rotten?

EIRNS/Stuart Lewis

"We have regular events ... in terms of the revival of Classical musical compositions' performance." Here Bach's Magnificat being performed at a Schiller Institute "New Paradigm To Save Mankind" conference in New York City in 2013.

But you know that most members of the electorate will vote up and down for the worthless ones. Most of the people that are voted for, are not fit to be voted for! And yet, that is the choice—you ask me to make a choice, who am I going to support? You think I'm going to support a jerk? Or a guy who doesn't know what he's talking about? A guy who has no conception of what the principles are on which the progress of mankind depends?

And I know that virtually *no one*, on this planet has an efficient conception of what mankind needs. They don't; they believe in something, but it's only imaginary. It's something they hope is true, but I know in general it's not true.

So the problem is, how do we get people to let go; stop believing that you have the makings of all the truth of mankind or something like that. You don't. All of you, because you were born within this generation or series of generations now, because most of you believe that your generation was right. Now, your generation was not always wrong; but it was very often right.

And therefore, these kinds of things, these kinds of complexities, when people get too eager to say that they know what has to be done and they need to have some-

one up there and hammer through the truths, as if by an act of force,— it doesn't work.

The basic thing, you know, about mankind is love, human love; human love of humanity; the love of creating a kind of mankind in the next generation which is better! Better to behave than anyone in the present generations.

And I'll tell you, also, most of the recent generations, in the Twentieth Century and Twenty-first Century were pretty much idiots when it came to morals and judgment.

So there has to be a revival, and it's going to come through a crisis, by mankind, by people going through a crisis. And people meeting each other, and saying *"We were damned fools!* We've got to make it right. We've got to get this thing right, finally!"

Look at the entertainment. Look at what people like for music, or what they call "music." What they like in terms of all kinds of entertainment, in terms of what they consider good taste: All of this is garbage! The education they receive from universities is mostly garbage.

But there is a truth and there's an accessible truth. But you've got to get a little more humility. And don't assume that just because you *believe* in something, that it's right.

The Nuclear War Threat

Question: This is D— from Arizona. I was at a meeting on Monday where they played an Alex Jones conversation with a gentleman, in which the gentleman said that they will not remove Hillary because Hillary has threatened to put out all the dirty linen on everybody if they ever attempt to indict her, and he predicted that Hillary, even though she's done a multitude of crimes and bad things, will never be indicted because of her threat to expose the criminality of everybody else. Have you heard that? And what are your thoughts on that?

LaRouche: Well, I say that's nonsense. That is not the truth.

Look, I know her. I know her, and I've had a discussion with her at the time that she began to turn her course into that of Obama.

Now, what happened was, she asked that I give some advice to her, to try to make things clearer to the people at that time. And I answered; I was happy to do that. But then, the next thing that happened of significance, was that she was hammered by the gangsters from Chicago, and she was actually threatened physically; and the import was the threat. And the gang from Chicago made the threat, it was made on behalf of Obama and the Obama Administration.

What happened was, in some way which I did not actually trace out, she turned. And she jumped on the side of the Obama Administration. Since then, she has been an Obama agent, in every degree, in every way! There could be no one so low, as to be as low as she has reached, in her departure from what her original intention had been. She's a stooge. We know about this thing: Obama is a killer. He's a mass killer. He kills people on Tuesdays, human beings, Americans: He kills them! People of great prestige, public prestige are terrified by the threats of Obama, just like Hillary.

How did she change, how did she become the animal that she acts like so often? She's terrified! She thinks he's going to kill her. And in that persuasion, that's a very likely fact. It could happen. But by whom? By Obama!

You've got to understand what history is: Obama as the President of the United States could be the death of civilization as a whole. *Get this guy out of office, if you want human beings to live.*

Don't blame her. Yes, she's acting like a bum, but *why* is she acting like a bum? Because *she's terrified.* And I don't know if her friend there is of the same persuasion.

Ascher: OK, Lyn, I just wanted to ask, because no one has explicitly touched on it, but since you were just indicating the danger and had put out several statements on this earlier this week, how would you assess right now the heightened danger of thermonuclear war, in the aftermath of what has occurred over the course of the immediate past period?

LaRouche: There is no magnitude as such, which will measure the danger that involves. What exists now, to the degree that the British Empire, the Monarchy itself, whatever else is in the British system, the Monarchy is the real Satanic factor in this thing. We are in a period in which a Satanic threat exists. Can we stop it? Well, I think what we're doing, we're trying to spend everything we can, in terms of efforts, to make sure that mankind survives. I know that in principle, Obama must be removed from office immediately, and some of his sidekicks should be thrown into the junk yard at the same time.

That given, I think the very fact that Obama was removed from office by action of the Presidential system would be sufficient change to get people to say, "Oh! I was terrified. I was terrified!" And when people sometimes act under pressure of terror, when that happens, then sometimes people come to sanity, because at the same time that they have a tendency to be, well, immoral, shall we say, when they are freed from terror, they tend to try to free themselves from their own bad habits as well.

And so therefore, I would say, we have to concentrate on the hope, that we are going to be able to get rid of Wall Street, just destroy Wall Street entirely; it has no use, it's a disease in and of itself. Besides it has no money value, either. And we can imagine, Wall Street has money, but the money is worthless, is worse than worthless. I mean, some people should get a little thought in their head some place about that: Why is it they believe in something which is inherently worthless? Or less than worthless?

So anyway, the point is that, perhaps, if we can do what we should do, we can induce enough of our fellow citizens and citizens of other nations to do the kinds of things that will put mankind back on the road towards civilization. We know that Russia is doing that; Russia is doing exactly that. China is doing that. The leadership of India is doing that.

So the situation is not inherently bad: The question is, can we get rid of Obama *and* the British Monarchy? Those two conditions, I think would be prerequisites for a new chance for mankind.

Escalating Toward World War III

by Robert Ingraham

Feb. 7—If they desire to live, well-meaning political leaders, military commanders, and the people of Europe and the United States must wake up from their self-imposed fantastical dreamworld. The ruthless crushing of the Martin O'Malley presidential campaign, an action taken by the Obama White House together with its masters in London and Wall Street, has now signaled a commitment by the British Empire and the Obama administration to rapidly escalate the war confrontation with both Russia and China. Everything which has happened so far—from Ukraine, to Syria to the South China Sea—is a mere prelude, a preface to what is now about to unfold. A terrifying scenario is upon us.

As Matthew Ogden characterized recent remarks by Lyndon LaRouche in the Feb. 5, 2016 LPAC Webcast, "the abrupt termination of the O'Malley presidential campaign, even before the final Iowa results were announced, was [a signal] that leading British circles, controlling the Barack Obama Presidency, are desperately escalating their preparations for war against Russia and China. The actions against O'Malley were, in effect, a red-dye indication of the war preparations already well underway. The fact that there were escalating British Crown provocations against Russian President Vladimir Putin, coincident with the actions against O'Malley, sealed the case."

The top-down decision to force O'Malley from the presidential race was taken mere days after Lyndon LaRouche had identified O'Malley as the only viable candidate around whom a new Presidency could coalesce, a Presidency whose first order of business would be to terminate the murderous speculative activities of Wall Street. It was the specter of a LaRouche-influenced O'Malley Presidency which forced the hand of Obama and his friends, and which has now catapulted them into a desperate flight forward.

Russian President Vladimir Putin with Chinese President Xi Jinping.

I. Casus Belli

Some analysts offer the opinion that it is the crisis and disintegration within the trans-Atlantic banking and financial system which is propelling Western leaders to opt for war. That is only apparently true, and ultimately represents misinformed opinion. Rather, there are two far more urgent considerations confronting the oligarchs and pseudo-oligarchs of London and Wall Street. The first of these is the reality of the catastrophic collapse of the productive economies of both Europe and the United States, a collapse that began in the 1970s but which has escalated non-linearly, since the repeal of Glass-Steagall, during the last fifteen years of the Bush and Obama presidencies. This collapse includes both an ongoing destruction of the physical economy, that is, industry, infrastructure, and science, as well as the destruction of the cognitive powers of the workforce, in terms of skills, education, and culture. The starkest example of this take-down of productive potential has been the almost complete annihilation of the remaining U.S. space program by Barack Obama.

This ongoing, escalating collapse of productive capabilities has created two problems for the forces of

"China has built over 12,000 miles of high-speed rail lines."

CC/Khalidshou

Empire. On the one hand, since the repeal of Glass-Steagall, the entire trans-Atlantic financial system has been transformed into a speculative house of cards, with gambling bets being multiplied daily and hourly, the whole multi-quadrillion dollar edifice of paper becoming ever more precarious by the minute. Yet, at the end of the day, those financial obligations rest on top of a physical economy which is disappearing and a workforce which is being driven into the ground. The physical means to sustain the gamblers' carnival no longer exists as of 2016. The U.S. and European physical economy—and the humongous financial parasite which feeds off of it—is going, going, gone. In response to this reality, some people will jump out of windows; others will go to war.

The second, and from the imperial viewpoint, more urgent problem associated with the collapse of the trans-Atlantic economy is that, simultaneous with this process of western physical decay and death, the world has also witnessed the explosive economic and scientific emergence of Russia and China, as well as several other nations associated with them through the BRICS, the Shanghai Cooperation Organization and the Chinese "One Belt, One Road" policy. China, Russia, and their allies are now surpassing the West in terms of manufacturing, energy production, basic science, and space technology and exploration, and this gap is widening rapidly. The reality that a new China/Russia-led world is coming into existence—a world directionality

which is increasingly determined by this explosive growth of productive potential—is a mortal threat to the interests of the British Empire and Britain's self-obsessed puppet Barack Obama. A future world, wherein the outlook of the win-win philosophy of Xi Jinping becomes hegemonic, is a world in which the British Empire will no longer exist and the oligarchical outlook will be obliterated.

To put the reality of the strategic disparity into tangible terms, consider:

China is now the largest manufacturing economy in the world, with a 22% share of manufacturing activity. The United States is in second place with a 17.4% share. Between 1992 and 2012 China has gone from 7th to 1st place; Russia went from 17th place in 2002 to 7th in 2012; and India went from 16th to 9th place. During this same period, manufacturing output in the United States, Canada, Britain, France, Germany, and Italy dropped, and dropped precipitously in some cases.

In 2000, the United States produced 102 million metric tons (mmt) of steel. China, India, and Russia combined produced 214 mmt. By 2014, U.S. production had dropped to 88 mmt, while the production of China, India, and Russia leaped to 1,001 mmt, a 500% increase. China now produces ten times as much steel as the United States. (An even starker picture emerges if one looks at the 1967 figures, when the U.S. produced 115 mmt, and China and India combined produced only 20 mmt.) As of 2015, the United States is now the largest steel importer in the world.

There were almost 18 million Americans employed in manufacturing jobs in 1998 (already substantially down from the post-World War II peak in 1979 of 20 million). By 2010, this figure had declined to slightly over 11 million, a decline of more than 35% in twelve years. Despite the much ballyhooed Obama campaign (and its phony statistics) to bring manufacturing jobs back to America, this picture has not changed in the last six years. Seven million American factory jobs have simply vanished in the "post-Glass-Steagall era" since 1999, many from the most advanced U.S. industries and machine tool sectors. Today, "public services," as well as finance, insurance, and real estate all surpass manufacturing in employment.

Even more dramatic has been the ongoing decay and collapse in education, water delivery systems, electricity generation, transportation, and other crucial infrastructure in America. Space does not permit a full description of all of the particulars of this collapse in productive capabilities here, nor an examination of the ongoing destruction of the culture, cognitive levels, and productive skills of the American population. One has only to look at the possibility that Flint, Michigan, could soon vanish as a city due to the lead poisoning of its residents from untreated local river water, to gain insight into the current state of physical breakdown in the United States.

Meanwhile, since 2007—i.e., in only nine years— China has built over 12,000 miles of high-speed rail lines, with 7,000 additional miles planned for completion by 2020. In nuclear technology, in addition to China's already operating 31 nuclear power plants, there are now 23 more plants under construction, which will bring the total to 54. Additional reactors are also planned, including some of the world's most advanced. China's current Five Year Plan includes provisions for building six to eight new nuclear power plants a year up to 2020, at which time it will increase to ten new plants a year.

In the field of nuclear fusion, on Feb. 3, 2016 China's Institute of Plasma Physics reported that experiments on its EAST superconducting tokamak had successfully created a sustained hydrogen plasma for a record 102 seconds. The goal of EAST is to reach 100 million degrees in the plasma and operate for 1,000 seconds, towards an eventual steady-state operation, which will be required for commercial fusion power production.

Space Exploration and the Galaxy

As LaRouche PAC leader Kesha Rogers has declared, in terms of a national policy orientation that provides the platform for the future generation of new scientific and productive potentials, the greatest crime of the Obama administration has been the take-down of the U.S. space program. When Obama ended the Constellation Project in 2009, he effectively terminated the fifty-year U.S. space effort.

On Feb. 3, 2016, the same day as the breakthrough in fusion energy research was announced, China's Aerospace Science and Technology Corporation announced that China is planning its next manned space launch, the Shenzhou-11 mission, for later this year. Also, in 2016,

China will launch its second orbiting module, Tiangong-2. The Tiangong series is designed to develop and test the technology that will be needed for the full-sized, manned station in the next decade. There will be further test launches of China's rockets this year, including the heavy-lift Long March 5, which is needed to launch the station modules and other heavy payloads, and the medium-lift Long March 7, which will launch the future unmanned cargo vehicle, Tianzhou.

Earlier this year, on January 14, China announced the Chang'e-4 mission, a project to land a rover on the far side of the Moon, possibly as early as 2018 (see accompanying articles in this issue). Another lunar mission, the Chang'e-5, is scheduled to land on the Moon in 2017 and return lunar samples to Earth.

Meanwhile, the Feb. 3 issue of *Popular Mechanics* reports that Russian engineers are creating increasingly detailed designs for a future manned lunar lander.

Let there be no unclarity. These Chinese and Russian space efforts represent the future of the human race, because they represent what the human being actually is, in his innermost nature, as different from and opposed to any animal. Discoveries about the processes of our solar system and our galaxy, new scientific breakthroughs, new technologies and inventions that can revolutionize human affairs on Earth—this endeavor is now being aggressively pursued by China, Russia, and their friends. If allowed to develop, this future will leave the institutions and axioms of the British Empire in the dustbin of history.

The Bigger Issue for the Monarchy

Please take note: None of what has been discussed so far is occurring in a timeless vacuum. To understand "the why and the how" of how world events are proceeding, it is absolutely necessary to view the current state of affairs through the eyes of the last three to four generations of British oligarchs.

Beginning in 1900 Bertrand Russell authored a battle-plan, on behalf of the British Empire, to put the "Renaissance Genie" of human development back inside the lamp. Together with his allies, such as David Hilbert, Russell launched attacks on Gottfried Leibniz, Bernard Riemann, Albert Einstein, and others. His intention was to destroy the Renaissance tradition in science and to impose a linear, logical view of the universe, one in which human creativity—that is, actual human nature—is deemed not to exist. Russell's view is that of the Malthusian British imperialist, of the type that has always hated the human species.

This is not simply a topic for scientists or mathematicians. The Florentine Renaissance of Brunelleschi and Cusa had created the culture from which the founding of the United States of America sprang, and the "republican virus" of the American Revolution had led, particularly after the Union victory in the U.S. Civil War, to the spread of American Ideals throughout the world. The Russia of Alexander II, the Meiji Restoration in Japan, and—most importantly—the Germany of Bismarck all represented, in their own ways, the American policy to eradicate the bestiality of Empire.

en.wikipedia.org
German Chancellor Otto von Bismarck, Lincoln's ally.

Russell's job was to turn back the tide. Joined by others, such as H.G. Wells and Prince Philip, Russell battled throughout the Twentieth Century to destroy science, destroy classical culture, and to impose a policy of worldwide population reduction which would end human progress forever.

Unfortunately for the Monarchy, things don't always go their way, as seen in the case of Franklin Roosevelt or the Soviet Union's victory over Nazi Germany. And things are not going their way right now. If the progress and optimism engendered by China and Russia are allowed to proceed, rule by empire is finished. Yet, the British, with their puppet-on-a-string Obama, are fiercely committed to their own agenda, the agenda defined by Russell. They will not yield. Thus, the stage is set. The drama proceeds. It is not that everyone wants world war. But that, most certainly, is the trajectory. Blunders, bluffs, and miscalculations will all add to the danger.

II. Financial Armageddon and Rearmament

Since January 1, 2016, that is, within just the last 38 days, major U.S. and European bank stock values have crashed by more than 30%. On February 1, the German financial mouthpiece *Handelsblatt* declared that "Deutsche Bank is in a free-fall," adding that the real center of the collapse of European finance is not on the periphery, i.e., Greece, Portugal, or Spain, but is centered in Germany and France, the industrial heartland of Europe. One financial publication estimates that Deutsche Bank, the largest foreign exchange dealer in the world, is sitting on a pile of debt that is 70% "impaired." On Feb. 4, the *Frankfurter Allgemeine Zeitung* reported that Black-Rock and Qatar, the two largest shareholders of Deutsche Bank, might pull out if things get worse. Other institutional investors have long since sold their shares. Union Investment, a German fund owned by the Raffeisen (cooperative) banks and credit unions, has halved its Deutsche Bank equities and warns of investing in shares altogether. One analyst stated that European leaders are now desperate to hide the actual nature of the crisis, "the real European problem: a giant financial black hole being created in Germany." Deutsche Bank alone holds 64 trillion Euros of derivative investments, five times the GDP of the 19-country Eurozone.

The banking sector on both sides of the Atlantic is crashing down. While Deutsche Bank shares have fallen by 35%, those of Citicorp have sunk by 22%, Goldman Sachs by 6%, JP Morgan Chase by 14%, Morgan Stanley by 23%, Bank of America by 22%, and Credit Suisse by 22%.

As financial expert Claudio Celani reported in the Feb. 5, 2016 issue of *EIR*, on Jan. 26 the entire European banking system came within a hair's breadth of collapse, which was only prevented by a decision of the European Commission to allow a bail-out of bad Italian bank loans, in violation of its own explicit rules.

As to the real physical economy, in the United States, mass layoffs in January were 42% higher than in January 2015, and a whopping 218% more than in De-

Deutsche Bank, "a gigantic financial black hole."

cember 2015. Retail cut the most jobs, with 22,246 announced mass layoffs—a seven-year high—and the energy sector was a close second, with the 20,246 mass layoffs. Texas was the state worst hit in the nation, followed by Arkansas, Ohio, and Virginia.

Meanwhile, the January monthly survey by the U.S. Federal Reserve of loan requests from the manufacturing and commercial sector shows a dramatic decline—more than 11%.

On the Hair Trigger

On Feb. 2, U.S. Secretary of Defense Ashton Carter delivered a speech to the Economic Club of Washington, a speech wherein he presented what can only be characterized as a military budget for World War III. Naming both Russia and China as the two primary strategic threats to the United States, Carter announced that the Obama administration will be requesting $3.4 billion for the "European Reassurance Initiative," way up from the current $789 million, to fund an expanded U.S. military presence in Europe, more training, more exercises, and more pre-positioned equipment, all designed to "respond theater-wide if necessary." At the same time, the Carter/Obama budget plan also calls for

$13 billion for a new ballistic missile submarine over the next five years, to replace the current fleet of Ohio-class submarines, and it stresses the need to fund all three legs of the U.S. strategic deterrent "triad"—not only the new submarines but also new nuclear-armed intercontinental ballistic missiles and a new bomber for the Air Force.

Other Obama Administration spokesmen have also emphasized that it is the targeting of Russia and China, not the "war on terror," which dominates what passes for thinking in the White House. On Feb. 4, an interview with Obama's Director of National Intelligence, James Clapper, was broadcast over all major TV and radio outlets in the Washington, D.C. area. Clapper bluntly declared, "ISIL is not a mortal enemy of the United States. It causes harm and can kill our people. But it can't inflict mortal damage to the United States. Russia can." He stressed the nuclear capability "that could render great harm to this country," and warned that Russia is "on a very impressive campaign to modernize its military in all its dimensions."

On Feb. 4, Obama's lapdog, the bitch-in-heat Hillary Clinton, went all in for a confrontation with Russia. Asked about Defense Secretary Ashton Carter's plan to massively build up advanced nuclear military forces on Russia's borders, Hillary said, "What Secretary Carter is looking at is the constant pressure that Russia's putting on our European allies. The way that Russia is trying to move the boundaries of the post-World War II Europe. The way that he [Putin] is trying to set European countries against one another, seizing territory, holding it in Crimea. Beginning to explore whether they could make some inroads in the Baltics... We've got to do more to support our partners in NATO, and we have to send a very clear message to Putin that this kind of belligerence, that this kind of testing of boundaries will have to be responded to. The best way to do that is to put more armor in, put more money from the Europeans in so they're actually contributing more to their own defense."

On the same day as the Clinton speech, the Turkish government, in defiance of the Open Skies Treaty, blocked a Russian crew from flying an observation flight over Turkey. The next morning, Russian Defense Ministry spokesman Major General Igor Konashenkov tied the Turkish refusal to evidence that shows Turkish troops are in the midst of preparations to invade Syria. Konashenkov stated, "The Russian Defense Ministry regards these actions of the Turkish party as a dangerous precedent and an attempt to hide the illegal military activity near the Syrian border. Moreover, the Russian party has reasonable grounds to suspect intensive preparation of Turkey for a military invasion of the territory of a sovereign state—the Syrian Arab Republic." Russia is in possession of a video that shows the Turkish military shelling Syrian territory using heavy artillery positioned close to the border. Konashenkov stated, "This is what we call a fact. This is irrefutable proof that Turkish armed forces shell borderline Syrian settlements with large-caliber artillery systems."

Escalation in the region is not merely coming from Turkey. Recent decisions have been announced by the Obama administration to send more troops and military equipment to both Iraq and Syria, which in the case of Syria is a direct violation of both Syrian sovereignty and international law. Additionally, on Feb. 5 the government of Saudi Arabia announced its desire to send ground troops to Syria to aid the anti-Assad "rebels" in their efforts to topple the Syrian government, an action which would put them in direct military conflict with Russia.

Desperate diplomatic efforts to diffuse the escalating conflict—most particularly those of U.S. Secretary of State John Kerry and Russian Foreign Minister Sergei Lavrov in pushing forward Syrian peace talks in Geneva—are being sabotaged by Obama and Obama's controllers in London. Under direct pressure from Obama, Kerry's State Department was forced to add five names to the so-called "Magnitsky List"—a list of leading Russian individuals sanctioned by the U.S. government for supposed human rights violations. This act, a blatant affront to Putin and the Russian government, came just days after the Treasury Department issued the scurrilous attack on Putin personally, as "corrupt," and the simultaneous release in London of a judge's report which states that the 2006 death of Alexander Litvinenko was "probably" ordered directly by Putin. All of this is intended by the murderer Obama and Buckingham Palace to poison the well in Geneva and destroy the peace talks.

On the Other Side of the World

On Feb. 1, *Global Times*, a publication put out by *People's Daily*, the newspaper of the Chinese Communist Party, published a lead editorial warning that the United States is preparing for war, nuclear war, against China. It called for China to "accelerate its speed of building up strategic strike capabilities, including a nuclear second-strike capability."

U.S. Air Force photo by Staff Sgt. Siuta B. Ika

U.S. Secretary of Defense Ashton Carter

The *Global Times* editorial references the U.S. deployment of a warship within the 12-mile limit of one of its islands in the Xisha (Paracel) Islands on Jan. 30, noting that this is not an unoccupied island, nor an artificially created island, but rather the Zhongjian Island "under China's actual control, and China has released the territorial sea baseline of the Xisha Islands, including Zhongjian Island. Therefore, the U.S. provocation this time is more vicious." The editorial goes on to state that this violation of Chines territory by the U.S. military has to be seen within the context of both the ongoing U.S. military occupation of the Philippines as well as a direct threat to the enormous sea trade by China through the South China Sea.

On the same day as the appearance of the *Global Times* editorial, Chinese President Xi Jinping participated in a grand inauguration ceremony in which he awarded the ceremonial flags of the five reconstituted military theaters. After the singing of the national anthem, President Xi spoke, saying, "The establishment of the five theater commands and their joint operational institutions is of great and far-reaching significance in ensuring the People's Liberation Army to be capable of fighting and winning battles and effectively safeguarding China's national security" Xi said the move to establish the theater commands and form the joint battle command system is a strategic decision by the Communist Party of China (CPC) Central Committee and the Central Military Commission aimed at

Igor Konashenkov, head of Press and Information of the Russian Ministry of Defense of the Russian Federation.

creating a strong military. He concluded by stating that the Chinese military should "always be prepared for war, so as to safeguard China's national sovereignty, security and development interests."

III. History to Consider

In his autobiography, *Marshal of Victory*, General Georgy Zhukov documents how the invasion of the Soviet Union by Nazi Germany in June 1941 was an action taken, to a large degree, out of fear, weakness, and desperation. By 1941 the economy of the German Reich was collapsing, held together largely by slave labor and raw materials looted from conquered territory. German industrial output actually declined from 1936 to 1940. The ability of the Hitler government to fund and resupply the German military regime was actually disappearing. Despite intensive efforts by the British ruling class to entice Germany into attacking the Soviet Union, almost all of Hitler's military advisors warned that this was a war Germany could not win.

Conversely, between 1938 and 1941, Soviet industrial output overtook and surpassed German production. The same is true for military armament. By 1941 the Soviets were outproducing Germany in tanks and other key equipment, and the gap was growing. The newer Soviet tanks and aircraft were also superior to their German equivalents. By June of 1941, the situa-

tion facing Hitler—in regard to going to war with Russia—was essentially "now or never," as any further delay would only increase the growing gap in industrial and military capabilities.

A very similar situation existed in 1914. Between 1880 and 1913, German coal production increased by 400%; steel production increased 500%; German rail lines increased from 5,000 km to 47,000 km; 50% of all European electric power generation was in Germany; other German manufacturing increased by 500%. A physical-economic-scientific power was developing that posed a direct threat to the global hegemony of the British Empire, an empire whose power was waning, and one which was largely sustained through colonial wars of extermination, drug-trafficking, and financial speculation. It was the growing weakness and fear within the Empire which impelled it to act.

So today, we see the collapse of the trans-Atlantic region proceeding apace with the industrial and scientific Renaissance emerging from China and Russia. Will London respond any differently than in 1914 or than as Hitler acted in 1941? Under the Putin leadership, over a relatively very brief time span, Russia has achieved a startling revolution in its war-fighting and war-avoidance capabilities. That includes new generations of military equipment and well-trained personnel. Even the top NATO maritime commander recently congratulated the Russians on the technological leap in their submarine warfare capabilities.

On Feb. 2, Russian Defense Minister Sergei Shoigu held a teleconference with the leadership of the Russian military leadership to review the progress of its modernization programs. The proportion of modern equipment in the Aerospace Forces has now reached 52%, with further deliveries of Su-35 fighters and Su-34 bombers, and Ka-52 and Mi-28N strike helicopters. They also discussed the resumption of production of Tu-160 strategic bombers and the implementation of automated planning systems and programs to improve the manning of the armed forces in general, among other things.

Reviewing the staggering accomplishments of this effort for military modernization, one is struck forcefully by the similarity to what was accomplished under Stalin from 1938 to 1941.

Responses to these developments from U.S. military analysts have been somber. Russia's submarine fleet is now particularly feared, much more so than during the Cold War, when the Soviet Union had many more submarines. NATO submarines are seeing "more activity from Russian submarines than we've seen since the days of the Cold War," Royal Navy Vice Admiral Clive Johnstone, commander of NATO's Maritime Command stated in an interview. He added that NATO submarines are encountering "a level of Russian capability that we haven't seen before ... the submarines the Russians are building are much better than anything they had before ... Russia has made technology leaps that [are] remarkable, and a credit to them."

General Georgy Zhukov and General Dwight Eisenhower.

Johnstone's comments followed, by days, an article in the Jan. 31 London *Independent*, which reported on the "shock" felt by Western military leaders who expected Russia's military deployment to Syria to fail in short order, but instead have watched the Russian military sustain a complex operation at a high operational tempo for four months now. "Russian military jets have, at times, been carrying out more sorties in a day in Syria than the U.S.-led coalition has done in a month," the *Independent* reported. "The Russian navy has launched ballistic missiles from the Caspian Sea, 900 miles way, and kept supply lines going to Syria. The air defenses installed by the Russians in Syria and eastern Ukraine would make it extremely hazardous for the West to carry out strikes against the Assad regime or Ukrainian separatists."

*   *   *

The American and European physical economies and productive capabilities are in a shambles, declining and dying day by day. The trans-Atlantic banking system and financial empire of derivatives is at the point of vaporizing. What will Obama do? What will Queen Elizabeth do? What do you think they might do?

Lyndon LaRouche stated during his Feb. 4 national Fireside Chat:

The question is this: There's things we don't know, but they are going to happen anyway. But we just have a lack of certainty among some issues, because we're not in an effective place to take on everything all at the same time. But there's no question that those of us who are intent on surviving this situation, surviving this period of history, are going to work with us, because it's the only way we have available, to do any good.

I'm not being pessimistic at all, because it's possible that we could bring off, which would actually shut down some of the things that are actually being put into place; it's possible. What we have to do, is concentrate on those conceptions, those options which do exist, and concentrate our attention on those options which we know are of a type which would be perfected, rather than trying to swarm around and trying to feel your way through the darkness. I don't believe in feeling through the darkness. I believe in finding loopholes in which we can make a progress.

It's like the military thing, you know; troops were out there on the field sometimes, waiting for the signal to enter combat, and it probably didn't happen at that time. But the point is, whenever this thing is in place, whenever it's in place as it is now; and then you have to react accordingly. And I'm ready to react accordingly.

There are things that can be done, which should be effective, in dumping Obama from the Presidency of the United States. That is the only thing, which will save the United States from self-destruction. So that's what I'm working on, and that's what I'm concentrating: It's the only thing that could work, and should work.

The British Monarchy and The Zika Virus

by Debra Hanania-Freeman

Feb. 8—These days, one would be hard pressed to find a news or media outlet anywhere that didn't feature alarming headlines concerning the rapid spread of a virus that garnered little attention just a short time ago. But on Feb. 1, World Health Organization (WHO) Director-General Margaret Chan, MD, declared the current Zika outbreak, which has been tied to an explosive increase in birth defects, particularly microcephaly, to be a "public health emergency of global concern." It is the same designation that was given to the deadly Ebola outbreak two years ago. Within a week of Chan's declaration, more than 29 nations and territories declared states of emergency, and that number grows daily.

Critics wondered what, exactly, was going on. Many thought Chan, who had been sharply rebuked for the WHO's slow response to the Ebola crisis, might be acting more out of concern for her own reputation than the situation warranted.

The criticism was based on the fact that, historically, Zika has never been considered to be a clinically serious infection. According to the U.S. Centers for Disease Control, roughly one in five individuals with the

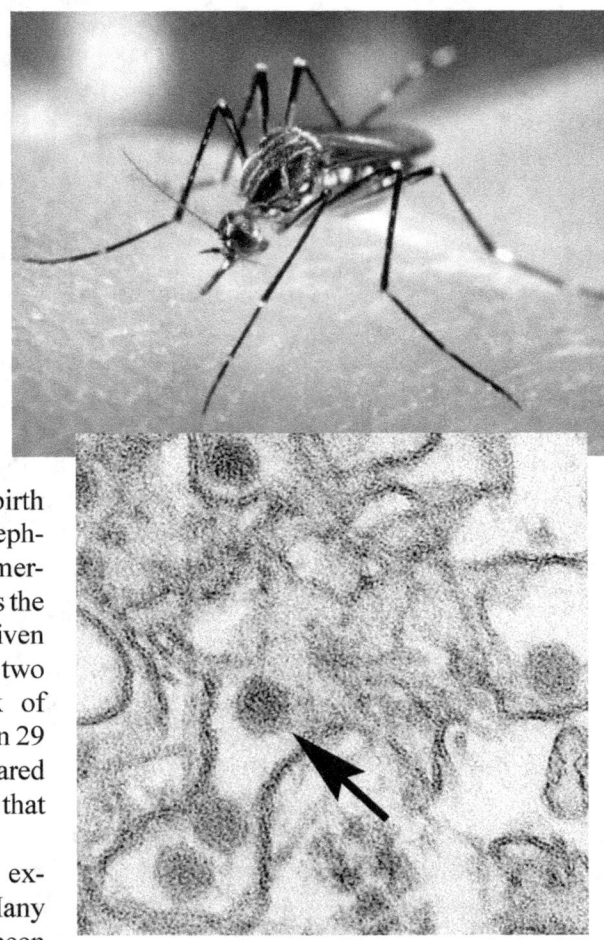

mosquito: wikimedia commons; zika virus: CDC

The arrow points to a Zika virus particle in this image from a transmission electron microscope. Top: the mosquito Aedes aegypti, *which spreads dengue fever, Chikungunya, and Zika virus.*

virus develops symptoms such as fever, rash, joint pain, and conjunctivitis, and those symptoms generally disappear within a week, and almost never land anyone in the hospital. During her press conference, Chan agreed that the virus alone would not justify a declaration of emergency, but said that the declaration was based on the fact that "a causal relationship between Zika virus infection and birth malformations and neurological syndromes is strongly suspected. [These suspected links] have rapidly changed the risk profile of Zika, from a mild threat to one of alarming proportions." Chan continued:

WHO is deeply concerned about this rapidly evolving situation for four main reasons: the possible association of infection with birth malformations and neurological syndromes; the potential for further international spread given the wide geographical distribution of the mosquito vector; the lack of population immunity in newly affected areas; and the absence of vaccines, specific treatments, and rapid diagnostic tests. . . .

The level of concern is high, as is the level of uncertainty.

Clearly, understanding *why* this is happening is critical to assessing how to deal with it.

Why Now?

Neither the virus nor the mosquitos that carry it came out of nowhere. It was first identified in Uganda in 1947, and is transmitted by the same type of mosquito that carries dengue fever, yellow fever, and chikungunya virus. A mosquito bites an infected person and then passes those viruses to other people it bites. Indeed, the *Aedes aegypti*, or yellow fever mosquito, killed more soldiers than guns did during the Spanish American War. Up until 2007, the Zika virus seemed to lie low, with only 14 cases actually documented, all of them in Africa. However, scientists suggest that this may well be due to the fact that the virus' symptoms are not severe and there is no actual test for infection. In 2007, the first major outbreak hit Yap Island in Micronesia. Other Pacific Islands began to see more cases, and in 2013, there was a significant outbreak in French Polynesia. The current outbreak in Brazil began in May 2015. It isn't clear how the virus got to Brazil in the first place, but the Brazilian government thinks a traveler to the World Cup may have brought it into the country in 2014, especially since it has been confirmed that the virus, although principally spread by mosquito, can in fact be sexually transmitted.

According to Carolyn McBride, a professor of evolutionary biology at Princeton University, who specializes in the *Aedes aegypti*, the mosquitos' ancestors lived in the forest where they fed on a variety of warm blooded animals. But some time in recent history, the modern *Aedes* mosquito developed a taste for just one target—human beings.

McBride explains, "They only live in association with humans And they have all these physical and behavior adaptions to do it. They have an amazing ability to recognize human odor and have adapted amazingly well to feeding on people."

Still, it would seem that the obvious solution would be to simply utilize DDT and similar insecticides to eradicate them, thereby dealing with the current Zika outbreak as well as the misery the insects cause passing on dengue fever, yellow fever, and Chikungunya from person to person.

McBride explained that, unfortunately, it's not so easy. "You have to first understand their habitat. On the one hand, they breed rapidly anywhere there is water. It doesn't have to be a lot of water. In Suriname, we identified 500 larvae in single discarded soda bottle caps. But, they don't have a lot of stamina in the air. Their flight range is just 300 to 600 feet. As a result, insecticidal sprays really don't work on this breed because in order to feed they have to stick to their intended targets (i.e. humans). It's very hard to catch them airborne." Although, she added, topically applied insecticides like DEET, do offer at least moderate protection.

But none of this explains the sudden explosive spread of the virus or the birth defects that seem to accompany it. The WHO estimates the virus will probably infect somewhere in the order of 3 to 4 million people during the coming months. In Brazil, unquestionably the epicenter of the outbreak, the explosion of the virus has also led to an explosion in the number of microcephaly cases—4,000 since October in a nation that saw less than 400 cases during the previous year.

What happened in 2015 that could possibly account for this?

According to a recent investigation by Claire Bernish published by theAntiMedia.org and other outlets, there was one very significant development in 2015.

Oxitec, a British bio tech company that specializes in insect control, unveiled its large-scale, genetically modified mosquito farm in Brazil in July 2012, with the goal of reducing "the incidence of dengue fever," as the *Disease Daily* reported. Dengue fever is spread by the same *Aedes* mosquitos which spread the Zika virus and though they "cannot fly more than 400 meters," WHO stated, they "may inadvertently be transported by humans from one place to another." By July 2015, shortly after the genetically modified mosquitos were first released into the wild in Juazeiro, Brazil, Oxitec proudly announced they had "successfully controlled the *Aedes aegypti* mosquito that spreads dengue fever, Chikungunya, and Zika virus, by reducing the target population by more than 90%."

Though that might sound like an astounding success—and, arguably, it was—there was an alarming issue these genetic engineers failed to consider: the impact of antibiotics in the environment caused by the heavy use in agricultural (animal feed) operations.

Bernish reports:

Only the male modified *Aedes* mosquitos are supposed to be released into the wild—as they will mate with their unaltered female counterparts. Once offspring are produced, the modified, scientific facet is supposed to "kick in" and kill that larvae [sic] before it reaches breeding age—if tetracycline is not present during its development... [That is, the presence of tetracycline overrides the genetically modified DNA.]

According to an unclassified document from the Trade and Agriculture Directorate Committee for Agriculture dated February 2015, Brazil is the third largest in "global antimicrobial consumption in food animal production"—meaning, Brazil is third in the world for its use of tetracycline in its food animals. As a study by the American Society of Agronomy explained, "It is estimated that approximately 75% of antibiotics are not absorbed by animals and are excreted in waste." One of the antibiotics (or antimicrobials) specifically named in that report for its environmental persistence is tetracycline.

The presence of antibiotics causes the mosquitos that are supposed to die off to survive and reproduce.

Warnings Ignored

As early as 2010, R.A. Steinbrecher of Department of Biosafety, Ministry of Natural Resources and Environment of Malaysia specifically warned against the release of these genetically modified mosquitos, warning that the 15% or so that survived could very well represent a subspecies of far more hearty mosquitos capable of reproducing more rapidly and possibly spreading more virulent strains of virus thereby worsening their spread. The same concern was apparently echoed in a confidential internal Oxitec document that was divulged in 2012. Additionally, Dr. Helen Wallace, director of GeneWatch, told the *Guardian* in 2012 that far more studies of possible side effects should be required before what she called superbugs were released into the environment. "It's a very experimental approach which has not yet been proven to be successful and very well may cause more harm than good," she said.

Jaydee Hanson, a senior policy analyst at the U.S. based Center for Food Safety, told Bloomberg News, "They're introducing genetic constructs that have never

creative commons/scorpions and centaurs

Zombies of the dying British Empire: Queen Elizabeth and Prince Philip on April 29, 2011. They have long sought drastic reductions in world population.

been there before. The mutated mosquitos are food for lots of animals. We still have to do studies of what occurs when birds and bats and amphibians eat these genetically modified mosquitos."

Not only were the calls for further study ignored, but today, Oxitec is offering to release a whole new set of genetically modified mosquitos to specifically target the Zika outbreak.

The question remains whether this Jurassic Park-type scenario was an accident caused by one company's irresponsible practice or not. The recent British television series "Utopia" suggests it could be a deliberate plan to reduce the global population.

The argument is certainly not without merit. The British monarchy has long advocated drastic reductions in the global population. It is also the fact that as early as the 1980s, Brazil, a nation with one of the largest black populations on the planet as well as the highest birth rate, was the target of a USAID program whose aim was to sterilize between 25% and 50% of the women of childbearing age in developing sector countries.

Indeed today, the rapid spread of the Zika virus across Latin America and its link to birth defects have prompted governments to do something that is almost unprecedented in human history: urge people to avoid having children. El Salvador has called for a voluntary moratorium on pregnancies until at least 2018. Brazil and Colombia, both Catholic countries, are asking women to wait at least several months, or perhaps indefinitely, before becoming pregnant. The United Nations has insisted that all bans on both contraceptives and legal abortions must be lifted immediately. Some have gone so far as to argue that lifting those bans in Catholic countries should be a prerequisite for the delivery of aid and support in dealing with the epidemic.

At this point, it is impossible to know definitively what is responsible for the Zika epidemic. There is a strong scientific and empirical argument to suggest that Oxitec's actions are at least partially responsible. But were they willful? Again, impossible to know now.

LaRouche's Forecast

As early as 1974, Lyndon LaRouche forewarned of the reality of an impending biological holocaust as a result of enforced primitive economic conditions imposed on the world's poorest nations by institutions like the IMF. He then set up a task force to study the biological-ecological breakdown and emergency of new diseases, and more virulent forms of old diseases, that were sure to ensue if the zero growth economic policies then being imposed were maintained. By the 1980s, such consequences were already unfolding.

On July 1, 1985, LaRouche's Biological Holocaust Task Force released an *EIR* Special Report titled, *Economic Breakdown and the Threat of Global Pandemics*, presenting handbook-style documentation of microbial disease threats. It detailed the scenario of a potential "biological holocaust," of new and re-emerging human, animal, and plant diseases, if economic growth policies were not restored. HIV/AIDS, then newly identified, was in the forefront. Today, almost 80% of the world's HIV/AIDS victims are in Africa.

Two years ago, the Ebola outbreak once again asserted this reality as it ravaged Africa's poorest nations, nations with no public health systems to speak of and only minimal modern infrastructure.

So, while many questions remain as to what accounts for this most recent epidemic, what is unquestionable is that it is being used to enforce policies of population reduction long advocated by the British monarchy and other elements of the Anglo-American financial establishment. Also unquestionable is the fact that the current rapidly escalating breakdown of the global financial system brings with it the spread of horrendous economic conditions and, unless it is immediately reversed, will result in waves of deadly, and in some cases, species threatening epidemics.